Before Dark

Also by Martin Anderson

The Kneeling Room
The Ash Circle
Heard Lanes
Dried Flowers
Swamp Fever
The Stillness of Gardens
Black Confetti
Belonging
Snow: Selected Poems 1981–2011
Interlocutors of Paradise
The Hoplite Journals
The Lower Reaches
Obsequy for Lost Things
Ice Stylus
In the Empire of Chimeras
A Country Without Names

Before Dark:
Collected Poems

Martin Anderson

Shearsman Books

First published in the United Kingdom in 2025 by
Shearsman Books
PO Box 4239
Swindon
SN3 9FN

Shearsman Books Ltd Registered Office
30–31 St. James Place, Mangotsfield, Bristol BS16 9JB
(this address not for correspondence)

EU AUTHORISED REPRESENTATIVE:
Lightning Source France, 1 Av. Johannes Gutenberg,
78310 Maurepas, France
Email: compliance@lightningsource.fr

www.shearsman.com

ISBN 978-1-84861-960-9

Copyright © Martin Anderson, 2025.

The right of Martin Anderson to be identified as the author of this work has been asserted by him in accordance with the Copyrights, Designs and Patents Act of 1988.
All rights reserved.

Contents

The Kneeling Room

Bamboo	17
Cockatoo	18
The Pressed Leaf	19
Flight	20
Chicken Itza	21
Schoolgirls	22
The Weaver	23
The Handsome Young Vendor of 'Stinky Bean Curd'	24
The Kneeling Room	25

Uncollected

Blackbird	29
The Pauses	30
To the Tune "Tao Lian Shi" by Li Yu	31
To the Tune "Lang Tao Sha" by Li Yu	32
Return to the Country by Tao Yuan-Ming	33
Icon	35
Pear	36

The Ash Circle

Horizon	39
Bridge	40
Oozedam	41
Distance 2	42
Dufy's *La Mer au Havre*	43
The Hollow	44
Giorgionesque	45
Rushes	46

Narcissus	47
Seurat's *Port-en-Bessin,*	
the Outer Harbour at Low Tide	48
The Old Russian Quarter, Harbin, North China	49
Snowy Owl	50
Logos	51
To Begin Again	52
Cacti	53
Fan Palm	54
The Church of St Mary the Virgin, Corringham	55
Peninsula	56

Heard Lanes

Herd Lane School	59
Orchid	61
Oasis	63
Fireweed	64
Heather	66
Fungus	67
Photograph of my Mother	68
Fossil	70
The Poem	71

Dried Flowers

An Urheimat	75
Gypsies	78
Fobbing	79
Tree Web Leaf River	81
'Esquire'	83
The Theft	84
In Exile	86
Twilight, Fruit Bat	87
A Kind of Love Poem	88

Driftwood	90
Dried Flowers	91
Dwarf Pine	93
Epitonium Dubium	94
At the British Cemetery	95

Swamp Fever

The Source	99
The Pumpkin by the River	100
Strata	101
Three Fathom Cove	102
Swamp Fever	104
The Tree	105
Tai Ping Shan	106
Russian Spring	107
Aurora	108
The Profligate	109
The Tallow Tree in Autumn	111
Early Traders in Southern China	112
Horace Edward Alston (1879–1953)	113
The Opium Smoker	115
Old Amahs	117
Girl with Bound Feet	118
To My Blind Student Reading	119
A Summing Up	120

The Stillness of Gardens

First Frost	123
House of Birth	124
Corringham	125
The Listener	126
Invasions	127
The Chase, Corringham	128

The Visitor	130
Words	131
Scribe	132
The Call	133
Meeting in Autumn	134
Waiting for My Father 1939–45	135
Bonfire	136
Chinese Red Pine	137
The Stroke	138
Near Bridge of Allan	139
The Release	140
Window	141
The Stillness of Gardens	142
The Destruction of the Summer Palace, Beijing 1860	143
Lotus	144
A Mute Inglorious Vegas	146
Indonesian Musicians at The World's Fair, Paris 1899	147
Émigrés	148
What's Left	149

BLACK CONFETTI

Snow	153
Post-Colonial Memorabilia	154
Holidays	155
Winter Monsoon	156
Clearing Customs	157
The Quay	158
Remedios Circle	159
The Garden	160
On an Unnamed Avenue at Evening	161
Every Window	162
Nightsong	163
The Kiss	164

Remains	165
The Amanuensis	166
A House on Remedios Street	167
The Home of Pain	168
The Flight	169
Spring, the Return	170
In Time	171
City	172
Mises-en-Scène	173
Of Christmases Past	174
Another Country	175
Lux in Domino	176
Maginhawa Street	177
The Stair	178
The Lovely Cow Dung Flower	179
The Past	181
Orchard Bungalow	182
Crepuscular Summer	183
At the 26th University of the Philippines' National Writers' Workshop, Baguio	184

Uncollected

The Fragrant Emporia	187
Between	190

Belonging

Light Where There Is	195
A Habitation	197
The Pear Tree	198
Edges	200
A Boyhood	203
Belonging	206
Archipelago Nights	211

City of a Thousand Lamaseries	215
Flume	217

Interlocutors of Paradise

The *English* Boat	223
City of Flowering Almonds	230
Ethnological Curiosities	236
Between the River and the Sea	243
The Bee Wood	247

Obsequy for Lost Things

The Lower Reaches	255
In the Year of Expeditions	262
Obsequy for Lost Things	267

Ice Stylus

Crooked Gulch	277
Ice Stylus	283
Unsubdued Singing	290

A Country Without Names

Rock Star Celebrates Birthday At Exclusive Country House Retreat	299
Road to the North	300
Alder	310
Driven Dust	317
Where No Snow Falls	318
Reliquary	326
Uncomfortably at Home	356

Road of Dust	358
Under Jui-yi Shan	363
A Country without Names	368
White Fire	375
When the Quinces Begin to Ripen	380
Flowering Midnight	384
From Tide Washed Salterns	392
The Carved Serpent	394
Night	396
Nostos	400
Acknowledgements	402
Notes	403

For Mohua

John Montague:
"Was there much of the journey you found worthwhile?"

Samuel Beckett:
"Precious little."

The Kneeling Room

(1981)

Bamboo

As you make a
pure line upwards
the air catches

its breath. Too
good for this world
that drags its

thorns and flints
beneath you. Yet
your roots are

twined darkly, and
grip, as you
climb into the

air, the clays, the
impurities. They lean
under the scarp

and twist. Driving
a knot into the heart
of the truly upright.

Cockatoo

Melting white
  snow, freshet
    of crest and

feather, from
  boulder to branch
    and into the

air, arabesque
  of water
    that the sun

slowly evaporates
  leaving a white
    trace only, a

vapour, thinning
  in the
    slag of air.

The Pressed Leaf

A leaf, clamped
between pages.

As I take it
out, it flakes

against the air
disintegrates. It

leaves, on both
pages, the print

of its teeth
holding its shadow

up. As, through
layers of rock

it appears
century on century, a

shape, that recurs
again and again

in the packed
layers of tissue

beneath the skull,
a shadow

haunting their
white folds.

Flight

Crash of
wings out of
foliage. Leaves

take off
flutter
the air. They

ripple along
branches
as if

its going
was a storm
calmly

lying down again.
In its nest
the two

white eggs
are cracked
are open.

Drops of
rain spin down
into it. Under

them, are
two drowned heads
with rinded eyes.

Chichen Itza

They raised the sun
here, on maize and

squashes, and put
up emblems in the

night, of sleek
eyed jaguar and

bat, to combat it.
When the cobs

fattened, and the jaws
gripped, they threw

out their hips, and
laughed. Then moved

them wider and
wider, in an

arc, a light on
the trampled grass

full of quetzal
and parrot feathers

enlarging the space
round their feet.

Schoolgirls

Shiny parabolas
you are fruit. The

undulate air
hangs round you.

Your brown luxuriance
your cottoned gift

exist in the
dull water about

your feet, your
socks turned up

against it, whiteness
measuring us.

The Weaver

*(my father at the mill at Balnamore,
Baile an Átha Mhóir, Antrim, 1921)*

His toes, under the
water, tapped dreamy
currents, and his
eyes traced the
irregular waifs of
vapour, slim as girls
floating into the vents.
He looked at them
through the window
tapering above the Bann,
An Bhanna, and there
in tawny rivulets
its tributary spawned
eels for him. His
eyes, in the fluid
sensual movement
danced. His hands
were lost, in
the slowly emerging
pattern that floated
on the loom.

The Handsome Young Vendor of 'Stinky Bean Curd'

On broken down
kerbs his spatula
clatters. In
his charred wok the
bean curd wrinkles.

When soft skinned
girls, mischief in their
eyes, lift it to their mouths
their faces moist
from summer heat

they sigh. On their
greased lips it slips
and trembles. It
begins to drip. Mouths open
their tongues lick

its white curdle, letting
it slide. As
he lowers his eyes
they grit their

teeth. Then
swallow. Their
faces pink
as if, laughing, they'd
just been kissed.

The Kneeling Room

Each time he entered
fraught with the
same longing, ache

its front porch shadow
exhaled an aroma
of jasmine. Against the

midday sun striking
the pavement were
pulled curtains heavy

as night. Its walls
became prayer-walls,
thinned by supplicants'

kisses; hollows developed
in its floor under the
weight of remonstrances.

Leaving it, none could
recall its exact location,
shape. Sometimes

a room he went into
suddenly reminded him
of it. And of the way

a shadow had always
covered its front
door porch, obscuring

house name, number.
Within it, an aroma
of jasmine made the

sun rinsed street swirl.
It said: "Enter. You
have been here before".

Uncollected

(1981–1983)

Blackbird

"The yellow billed blackbird
whistles from the blossomed whin"
(9th Century Irish)

That branch   bunched with gold
would heap its treasure on the
listener   if that bird   billed
with yellow   could unloosen the hold
on its throat of centuries   filled
with a tongue that is foreign

The Pauses

       Sound

 held   in the ear

      a curved

           insistent shape

the fondled

      neck of a

   jar   moving

  through

    the room   so full

     it seems

to break

     upon the tongue

with

      half of its weight

           else

       where

To the Tune: "Tao Lian Shi" *by* Li Yu

Growing deeper and deeper, my garden is quiet.
And the small courtyard is empty.
The cold beats in on a flurry of washing stones; the wind continues.
The long night shrugs its shoulders turns over, but doesn't sleep:
lies awake counting, till a thousand washing stones hammer the
    moon into the curtain.

To the Tune: "Lang Tao Sha" *by* Li Yu

Outside the curtain rain sighs down.
Spring: washed out word, feeling.
Fifth watch. Wind a knife through blanket.
In dream, forgetting the body was captive,
engorged with wine and music.

Alone in the evening. Lean on the balcony.
Rivers, mountains roll on and on, without limit.
What we're parted from dare not ask when again we'll meet.
Dropping flowers, rushing water. Spring. Gone.
Far. Unattainable country.

[Li Yu, 936-978 CE, was the last emperor of the southern Tang dynasty. Captured and taken north to the Sung capital and placed under house/palace arrest, he was forced to take poison for allegedly, in a line in one of his poems, appealing for the restoration of the Tang dynasty]

Return to the Country *by* Tao Yuan Ming

I

I was not born to the world's music.
My being was ground in hills and mountains.
For thirty years I breathed the din;
it toiled and choked me.
Trapped birds pine for the trees.
Pond fish long for wider waters.
In the south I broke open wild edges
returned to these hard farmlands
with ten or eleven acres, a house
and a few straw huts to sustain me.
Elms and willows flood eaves with shadow.
Out front the courtyard is full
of pear and peach trees.
A village greys in the distance;
a soft spoil of smoke hangs over its market.
Dogs bark deep in alleys.
Cocks crow in mulberry bushes.
These houses and courtyards
are deaf to the world's music.
A bare room accumulates space to think.
For years a net hung on my sight.
Now I return to what's within me.

II

Nobody of importance ever comes to this place.
Our dead-end lanes echo only to the rattle of one harness.
Doors stand half open in day's clear light.
In bare rooms thought gathers no dust.
In cloaks of woven straw sometimes, returning
from market, we meet in lanes.

When we meet we talk, but our talk is always free of gossip.
Mulberry and hemp keep it pure.
Every day the mulberry and hemp on my acres prosper.
Always, though, I am afraid that frost and hail
will level everything and drive me back to wild grass again.

[Tao Yuan-Ming, 372-427CE, the poet of quietness and solitude. Of his poetry the great Sung dynasty poet Su T'ung-Po wrote: "There is no poet I treasure more …He wrote few poems: they are plain yet beautiful, rich and yet not ornamented. Tu Fu, Li Po and all the others are inferior to him".]

Icon

         Light

  the   cracked skin

    Air   leaving itself

  through this rent

lighter   lighter

    pounded foil   embroidered

gold   sumptuousness

     attaining simplicity

          in this

 dry wind

       where

  the thistle   crucifies itself

(Parikia, the Cyclades)

Pear

                         Co-
    agulated   breath
                              blown
     through
the horizon   shower
              glittering
     threads
   woven through the eye
       out of
that dark   chimera
      effluvium
                that embrace
  Of the flesh   a
     continual
                fire

The Ash Circle

(1986)

Horizon

Curve

                transparency

    fold

                  of effulgence

air

      the mind

     closes on

                appetent

                          pre-

occupied

        Gloss

    that moves   through

      it

Bridge

      Confluence

of water   stone

      The eye's

   Silted penumbra

             Floats

Where we can't reach

  or hold

       Comes

through the air

            the dark

  tongue   Water

ing our etiolated evening

             Words

Oozedam

              Saltings
    wiers of silt
                          bleach
        ing stones
The river cracked
    to a dry whisper
    in the grass
Far out   the gleaming fleet
     withdraws
   light
         distance
     breaking upon itself
   like glass
        Under it
the vanished fields and walls
                     listen
     The forests of ash
  open their scars

Distance (2)

     At its petrified edge
        the tree
   can go no further
                    A furious white
breath   erases its leaves
        its rings
      At the heart
    of the stone   a mist
       spreads
              There are no doors
there   or windows
    Only   opening onto itself
      the mind
's terrified cry   The light
     of it   dispersed

Dufy's La Mer au Havre

    Deep blue   simulates

*

Mind   Restored
      to itself
    Its tremulous   mask
         its oils

*

                  Outside
two   blue klaxons
      blow   and pass

The Hollow

    Tight   in the eye's corner
       this gold   this beating
horizon   that's spawned
   further and further
     and   through the hollow
          the lust
  re at the tip of
the tongue   breathes
  in the rippled
corridor
   the palpitant room
an unease
       Grey as ash
    bright as fire
  within the walls
         Our unexcavated speech

Giorgionesque

Woven   through the flesh
    this gold dust
  this thread   In the black
    folds of the cypress
its filaments spin   They
    are pulled   through
  a white dusk
into this glistening rain   this
  vermilion   the 'ground
of the flesh'   that is breathing
  under the lip of
  the sarcophagus   into
    our name

Rushes

      In muscled
  air   the shudder of
     italic stems
                Tissue
in   its ambulant dress
                  Its super
   fluity
       (within the wind
     's wantonness)
           to which we
bend   Our other
    ness

Narcissus

   Feels   through each crease
    of water   his body ripple,
a shadow   heavy as
     stone.   Through his
   arms   in limpid light
it moves   a line of shivering
    gold   in the November
night.   Tightens
   round his heart   He steeps
     fingers in it.
And there   quivering
   is that flesh
   air is full of
   that lines his breath,
through which   he thinks
     and walks
          into no body
  other
     than his own

Seurat's *Port-en-Bessin,*
the Outer Harbour at Low Tide

                Silence

                                flat

       tened encomium

                                    flow

of escutcheon

          stone   latitudes

             emptying

   themselves   evacuated

            streets   the load

                 ed   horizontal

The Old Russian Quarter, Harbin, North China

    Tiered kokoshniki
draped with snow   Leftover
  borscht   The stones
of the streets point north

     In the silence
of deserted rooms   the striated breath
  of the crystal
forms   on walls

     Tremulous above pilastered domes
of a church   the eye of a glass angel
  in the grey wind off the tundra
slowly   thaws

Snowy Owl

    Two eyes   float
        on a tumult
of air   above a sharp
    -ly incised breath

                Feather and bone
     torn apart
drip   Through the trees
   lighter
  whiter   than an afflatus
      it rises   hiss
ing
          Around its neck
    small
  globules of blood   glisten
        Beneath
      them
twitching intestines
            freeze

Logos

Up and up it comes
through crushed granite
on this loosening
stammering
stairway of sound
It pauses
light
stepping through
a leaf
as it slides
through the tongue
and
with a rattle
of black quartz
and ashes
streams
in a white
humus
toward
the   stars

To Begin Again

The light of
    place the eye
 's light   The green
       pulling space
the secret snow   Behind us
they wait
         They fill
  with a cold
 aqueous light
        the stones
  They sing
under our hands
        They turn
 all of the afternoon
     all of our ruminations
  white

Cacti

The hoarded flesh beneath the
                                        spines
   The
succulence

whose weight
                in
        stone
  and
sand
        is
                slowly gathered

                    A
      small
          red
  flower   a coaxing
                        within
that dry
  abstemious purse
                Formal
                      admission
        of
       desire

Fan Palm

Cloud
of nothing
Embrasured
light
gleaning
Pulled
through itself
till
it's opaque
The
dream
of flesh
that's forever

fading
to
this

green nimbus

whisper

The Church of St Mary the Virgin, Corringham

    Beneath the sweet   and
layered antiphonal   snow melts

    femur of buck   and doe
in the rubble   of chancel walls

    crisp white bones   of herring
fall   ten centuries

    the uninterrupted light   ground
to a fine dust

Peninsula

In a rind
of shadows
the sediments
slip
On strands
beneath crackling
blue lakes
Perishable micas
evaporated schists

On the light
their hard residues
ache

Heard Lanes

(1989)

Herd Lane School

(In memory of Mrs Collier)

Light streamed
through warped glass
of the windows.
Wide
estuarine, it fell
onto the floor.
She stood in it
And read

The faraway tree
entered the book
In lanes
       we heard
ice crack,
gates drag
on furred hinges.
Frost-blooms
    thick
incurious on branches
moved
in the light
on pages

it snowed
She paused
A ghostly
  hiatus
          grew.
And, through it,

holding our breath
we heard
in cold air
the pond creak
in its dark reaches
as if it was searching
searching for a word

that would articulate
it draw it
   in
to the room
where desks gleamed
in deep glosses
and nothing,
as we hovered
above our reflections,
waiting,
   waiting
               nothing
   stirred.

Orchid

Fragile bloom
of the ephemeral,
above the lime tip
the bee bites
the voluminous tissue
of your lip
and mounts you;
rubs
until the seed grips
his back, then,
breathless/palpitant,
glides over the long luminous slide
of your shoulders
and leaves you.
In the summer's
deep fecundity of air
you wait,
ovary twisted
under a leaf,
for the amorous wind
to deceive
again and again
with your curves
and projections
to delicately pivot
him
    down
into your nectarious shadows
    there
to swim
against your stigma
   eyes covered
with the fine dust

of an infatuation;
   intoxicated,
               unable to rise.

Oasis

                    To travel
         towards it   s O
                    ripe
            upon the tongue
                        drinking
         its shadow
                    cool
      in the depths
               rising   falling
                to breathe
                through it
    fragrant oil   wet salt
                   fringed
            half oval
                         reified
    in the vowels'
              wide cleft
            fizz
                      sibilant
                 filling
    unravelling
            the soft   innermost part
                   of it
                self
         quenching   desire
              making it hiss

63

Fireweed

In ruins
of blitzed buildings
bombsites
you proliferate
forgiveness
deep sky blue
flower
without a sound.
Who,
through that high chronometer
counting
counting
as the bomb
fell,
could foresee
or hear
in the twisted catastrophe
of air
the minutes ticking
ticking
in your roots,
or
that chastened petals,
undulant
whorled
round your stem,
could unwrap
the heat
from that flash
in a deep wave
rushing
from the earth
and disarm it

with this bright purple
weed
replace it
with this fire
that can't be quenched?

Heather

Above the bleached grey podsol
it blossoms.
The hill
is awash in an afterglow
of minerals,
chrome
nickel and cobalt.

Anthers,
soft bells
on a wave
of intense blue,
through sandstone
    gravel
               loosen

the light
that in hard pans
burns up
through their dark roots.

    Reveal
the slow
       festering
of metals.

Fungus

Cracked sugars
melt
and burn under the rain.
A rippled moon
dances.
In the field
pure starches blaze
up
into a stem.
Pale headed
under the hand
their light.
Opaque
tightly drawn
skin
this rooted circle
grips
the hollowness inside itself.

Enters,
chanterelles
distilled
carbon,
the soft tumescence
of
the rain.

Photograph of my Mother

In the light's
shuttered immobility
you breathe

for this loved body
the air parts
its luminous shadow
and waves.

Amorous
funereal
halogens click.

Through the alchemy
of metals
a dry day
a still
centre
a voluptuous
music.

You pose.
The noise
of Time
bell/clock/watch
breaks
into your heart.

A hard
white gaze
emanates
from your hands
and feet.

Behind you
your bones
speak.

Fossil

The blue dust
of stars
in our bones,
rock,
a dark door
opening,
crumbling
among the lichens.
In a clear pond
the drowned molluscs
and the wasps
are falling,
and falling.
Free of us
at last
our bones tumble
down the long shaft
of our blood.
We listen.
At the dark
well-head
we cannot hear them
drop.

The Poem

In abandoned crania
of the wind
it grinds.
Dark,
and riven.
Gleams.

Through it
the fierce
cold light
off the escarpment
bottomless,
shadowless,
breathes.

At its heart
a hard
nacreous crystal
contracts.
Tightening
upon itself
it dreams.

Clear
steep slope
of air.
The curve of it
in the mind
Meta incognita.

Dried Flowers

(1990)

An Urheimat

Down washed out roads
they walked
into thin air,
they vanished.
Dark vocables,
obliterated voices.

.

Fierce wall of ice
upon the Taurus
mountains.
Clink of a cob's hoof
beneath it.
The unspoked wheel
turns and turns
the trundled cart
leaving behind it
such spaces;
wind blown escarpment
lake.

.

From field
to field
each glittering syllable
each culm
intact
in that slow wave
that advances.

.

What the hand transcribes,
pure white margin
drinking the weight
of these letters
one by one,
walking out of a high
Anatolian light.

.

Ghost of a word
under the tongue.
From its succulent stem
dem
domus
the *house*
rising.

.

Slender grey mouth
of stone.
Each consonant
and vowel wedged
against the dead
post frame
that rotted
and has gone.

.

Word
under the corn
feldspar
iron and bone.

Stippled bracken,
broom
where the burr
of the *r*'s sweet
on the air.
Bloom
through each deliberate
rustle
of sheath and glume.
Bring,
through tremulous ear
and tongue,
through this dark
spoliated tract
of migratings and siftings,
finally,
us home.

Gypsies

Through what broken lands
they move
rancour, and calumny,
their syllables pressed
against the air
of a dark migration
a continuous reproof.
In some green field,
concealed from the world,
they recount and dream
of an endless constatation
of roads, a journey. How it began
with nothing, and will end
with nothing:
the faded cinders of a circle
a faint depression in the ground.
Only their words (like smoke
in their mouths) marking,
down deserted lanes and tracks
and abandoned clearings
full of whittlings,
where they have been.

Fobbing

Marsh scrub:
flag and rush
bittern, plover.
Among it argent
and gule of Jute buried
under thick coverts
of thorn and gorse.
Here,
in the first assart,
among felled willow
and uprooted aster,
they raised a chapel.
Beneath its ragstone
and flint walls
unculled by wind, centuries
the bull-sedge
(*bula-secg*)
spreads.
Shaggy, bearded
upon banks
of slithering silt
it grips,
in its hard sound,
a rush
of haltered nasals and plosives
bound taut as withes.
With them they made,
above the cord grass
and the trapped salt,
here,
where their shadowy form
rasps and clicks

upon our tongue
still,
a second clearing.

Tree Web Leaf River

The river breathes
in its grey penumbra
beyond the tilted dark
curlicues of the trees.
There is a writing
on the window.
Syllables, sounds that have
not been heard before.
The tethering gold
of the web under the eaves,
the leaf's (pinned
to its shadow on the wall)
thin frail tributary
of veins, inscribe
the silence with
their names: the intricate
entablature that evolves
round them, potent
vibrating. Behind them,
at sloping desks, down
the long afternoons
of summer, stand doors
that open into the years.
A child steps through
them, pronouncing word
after word,
like a catechism, turning
the page of a gradual
and permanent erasure.
One day he will
look back, and try
to open them. To
touch, through the pale

residuum of its sound,
fricative and plosive
loose on the wind,
that grey, quivering
shadow again, faded cunabula
beyond the trees.

'Esquire'

Forlorn,
derelict,
brambles growing through
its trellis of
archaic sound,
up the crunching gravel
of the ear
by the wide lawn
it stalks,
under faded bunting
and flags.
Partridges haunt,
with plump grouse,
the soft moors
of its slopes.
From its lost halls
and dining rooms
the butler
and the valet call.
All the foxes stand,
as its shadowy catafalque
lurches past,
to attention.
Each one raises
a mauled paw.

The Theft

Stared into, never entered.
Behind the wrought iron gate,
the high stone wall.
Through summer after summer
the high chestnut swung
above it, and dropped
without a sound. Propped
on the wall he listened.
Behind the undulant wave
of lace, in the deep
bay window where the glint
of book-spines fired each wall,
their voices rose on a
sonorous curve, and fell.
Amid the delicate clink
of china he strained
to hear their low proprietorial
syllables form in long
involuted sentences. His breath
held. Plenitude of sounds,
of pauses, of the high
superordinate word. Through it
the coriander and the tall columbine
of the wide border twined
their stems, each species
and sub-species, *Camellia japonica
Punica granatum*, into his ear.
Silently, through long nights,
when snow fell against the doors
and windows and covered
the fields, and the clothes-
horse sweated in the front room,
he intoned them. Gradually,

week after week, month
after month, before the mirror
where he moved his lips
leafing the large lexicon
that he'd bought, nasals
that had been inaudible
were noticed, plosives
that were always unaspirated
exploded. Upon his tongue,
beneath high summer moons
among lanes, a clear mellifluous
water, a freshet of fricatives,
began to roll onto the air.
He smiled. Behind walls,
shrined in their arbours
before sundials, boughs
grew heavy with the golden
leafing of new words
and sounds, through which he drew
an intricate harmony, an
interlocking music. The rotundity
of its shadows enveigled his mouth.
And, from the deep garden,
he inhaled their scent.
Each slow, scrumped vowel
inscribed in the air
its perfect circle of breath
acqueous, vibrating.
A soft, voluptuous alphabet,
angel of letters and of impressed seals,
swam; an uncalumniated
dream of caramelised apples
                    inside his head.

In Exile*

"My children too have learned a barbarous tongue."
                                        Tu Fu.

At that fragile frontier of signs you stop,
and listen. Grief: at the heart ripped out,
the cranium gouged off on the roads. Chang'an.
As you lower your head to read the dusk
slowly expands across the river.
Snow falls, out of a dead sky. Poetry.
Crows tearing the flesh of horses
dead in the shafts, driven too hard, after
so many hurried farewells on the painted terraces.
Smoke devouring the city, where the lotuses
turned red all summer, where the censers never went out.
From dark alleyways and courtyards, now,
its noise drifts through the moon's pale light,
broken, cacophonous, across the river.
Above your desk the blood stained shadow
of the lotus moves its slow, ineradicable
wreath of leaves. You write.
In the snow's fallen silence, a hundred years
of the saddest news; a road for none but the birds.

* (In K'uei-chou on the middle Yangtse where Tu Fu went in 766 CE when the rebellion of An Lu-shan drove him south from the capital Chang'an)

Twilight, Fruit Bat

    As it descends
beside the lake
              it grips
the shadow
of a white
convolvulus
        devouring
leaf on leaf
the unpronounceable weight
of its name.
The faded signature
of a world
            we inhabit.
At its heart
    a thin mist
an echo.
An emptiness
    we cannot touch
  that would
            devour us.

    Beside the quay
an unanchored boat
    slowly   becomes
its own shadow.
The silence becomes
             the silence.

A Kind of Love Poem

In the pen's dark
recusant throat
you melt.

From the schism
you've drawn warmth

back
like a fire
to my hand

the petals
of a flower, skin's
soft glow
glabrous
taut
you are
this
sweet gloss
of air
of sound
dividing up

itself.
And
the magnet
which draws
through that slowly
devouring obsession

window, eye
what's out
side
hill, sun
star
all the parts

back.

Driftwood

In the frozen heart
    of a glacier
the top
    of a truncated fir
whitens, gleams:
    in an airless glaze
its twisted boughs
    held up
in an avalanche of crystal.
    They move
without moving,
    in that silent
windless place.
    As they lurch,
year by year,
    down the valley's
plundered slopes
    their fragile tendrils break
like glass.
    A floating effigy
with no leaves;
    a candelabra
that shakes.
    Over the deep
bedrock, in the vast dark
    of the basal ice,
it lights
    nothing.

Dried Flowers
(*i.m.* D.B.A.)

And nothing now
  to give you
more, or less,
  than was customary,
always,
  between us
than these
  so minutely proportioned
against the dark
  that consumes you
and memory and the light
  of the days –
attenuated
  taut peduncles,
calyxes of fire
  that will burn
on, without water
  rustling the tongue
of a cool
  unideological morning.
Naming for you
  such assurances and reassurances
that I speak
  and, in that activity, seek
the long looked for
  immobility, the repose
(not yours)
  of these flowers
that were wild once.
  That the heat dried
for your tears
  and to be

nothing if not curious
  angular to the touch
of light, of air.
  Turning each day
small, and smaller,
  the spaces of love
between us:
  until they are as rare
ified and pure
  as time is to us
for whom time is not
  ever to be
eradicated or abjured.

Dwarf Pine

    Sun burnt
fosse, dry rattle
   of pebble
above shale.
    Scarps tremble
under the grip
   of snow, ice.
They slowly rot,
   and are held,
where the eye
   gathers
them in cloud,
   and the long
limestone scar twists
   above the crevice's
jagged throat.
   On thin beds
of eddied sand,
   too,
bent grey
   stunted
the dwarf pine,
   in sheer shadow,
pushes
   small
immaculate
   yellow stamens
into cold air.

Epitonium Dubium

In the delicate weave
of water. Umbo.
A slow, chitinous skin
circles and circles
over bone
          white ribs.
In their thin staircase
the moon
          turns
a perfect spiral.   Held
between thumb and
forefinger, I listen.

On a far shore
a cold, dry lunar air
breaks, a pure intergalactic
shower of distances
and silence
          Breaks
like a sudden whorl
of snow. Then pauses.
In the deep white breath
of the caesura,   earth
    washes
      the moon's
                bones.

At the British Cemetery

Such lapidary light on a
name. How the name lasts
and lasts, incising the
sound of itself into
pure space and distance,
forgetting neither the day,
month nor year of its
inception, waiting
beneath crusted lichen
on crumbling stone
before that long
incurious line of those
who pass it, year after
year above a glittering
sea. Waiting: for the
one only who knows
with what a familiar
and importunate note
the tongue each day
once rolled round it.
It stumbles now, hand
scouring cloudy spores
in heat and dust, slowly
pronouncing each letter
as the eye teases out
before dark, for the quickened
pulse, a thin harvest.

(Hong Kong)

Swamp Fever

(1991)

The Source

Under hands
the stones palpitate
as if the heart was

in them. Primed
and pulsed at
the earth's core

a streak of red
granite runs through
them. The hands

touch it, fingering
like a spoor
its weaving dark.

The Pumpkin by the River

    Boughs turning over
you, water under
  you. You eat

  your heart out
like a flame
  as if to

  tell me. I
should know, from
  the heat in my

  hands, what it
is, what makes
  the flesh a vapour.

Strata

In strata
    torn like paper
the ferns move
    slow hands.
Calcite blows its
    white crustation
through their veins.
    Drop by drop
the years deposit
    into this silence
their shaley scuff.
    On each packed
layer they are
    bedding down. I
run my hands
    across them.
They stir.
    Then harden.

Three Fathom Cove

    Plunge the
mind in, through

    the grey
wave, to this

    wet pit.
Here, three

    fathoms down
in soft black

    shale, the flattened
fossils lie.

    Between each
dyke, in a

    deep sleep, they
coil, eating their

    bands of sediment
listening, year

by year, to
    the slow fall

    of the coast.
Their fine

    white skeletons,
their sharp

    edged teeth,
Cephalapsis, Iguanodon,

    wait to inherit
the earth.

Swamp Fever

Black against
the portico
at evening. No emanation

from the ground.
A swarm, slow
moving, drifts

through the open
slats, and eddies
in the whirr

of air from
the ceiling. Steadies
then draws away

to blunder against
nets. It departs
lifting through

the tall shutters
unheard above
the fans, leaving

a red mark
that will burn and
tease the brain

till, through
the long delirium,
the trees walk.

The Tree

The root is
knotted in
the bank, tied

through it
like a shoelace,
pulled, till the

clay has bulged
into it
bright as blood.

The limpid
green of leafage
shows nothing above.

A dark burl
whorls in
the trunk, thickens.

At its
centre, the light
springs out.

Tai Ping Shan

Nothing here
   except grey mist
      drizzling on rock.

A stone wobbles
   and is gone
      into the blankness.

I listen. No
   sound of it
      falling. Nothing.

Only the quiet
   knock of my
      heart, deflecting

off the bones
   of my ribs
      sternum, counting

as if it
   feared to be
      lost too, smothered

in this down
   suck of air
      and water.

Russian Spring

Each door in the house
gaped. You
broke in, immense and

yawning. They hammered
brackets, soaked the
wall outside with pitch

starred in a diurnal
explosion. Trees dragged
their roots, and neighbours

left vast chairs for you
and chattered under the
thatch. The water

butt drank dry the
canal, and the apples
turned red in the street.

Aurora

She flows
up bright against
tree and window
rattles the

garden gate.
A girl
so suddenly arrived
you rush to

hold her. Her
thin body in
a shift, legs
of table, arms

of chair.
Quietly she glides
on her soft
feet beside you

and leaves
no trace, except
red sheets, of
her being there.

The Profligate

Too softly they
enwound him, from

their knees to
their chins

drawing him in
to their perfumed

spaces, making
his senses swim.

The sliding torrent
of the body

took him.
Down, down

with it he went.
I used to poke

fun at him. Now
I ponder the descent,

as a young wife
ponders too imagining,

night after night
assignations and

faces. They drift
through walls and

doors, implacable
ghosts trailing their long

insomnias behind them.
They are bitter flesh.

The Tallow Tree in Autumn

In the afternoon
   the light

slips out
   of its gently

waving body
   and is gone.

Leaf and
   stalk are

buried in
   shadow. Inside it

the fat
   white seeds of

the capsules
   hold their own

candle, and
   the sugar pumped

sap reddens
   to a burn.

Early Traders in Southern China

Beneath camphor
    and banyan
in the bright
    sun, their names
'Jardine', 'McMurdo'
    incise the marble
with a burr.
    It rolls upon itself
like water.
    Their hard, metallic
eyes groan
    like the breakers
on that
    northern shore, grey
with its damp
    longing. Their
opiumed fingers are
    scutched white
as cloth.
    In denuded
linoleum parlours
    the sound
of a wasp
    keeps rising.
Night and morning
    it sucks
the pewter light
    above the door.

Horace Edward Alston
(1879-1953)

  At eighteen
on the Canadian
  Pacific, bound for
Saskatchewan, he drank
  most of his
allowance away in
  a bout of depression.
"Bottlenecks grew
  like thistles" he
said "on that long
  track. Everywhere
was desert". Dog
  tailed he came
back. On Tilbury
  Dock his father's
eyes blinked
  once: jaws set
into opposition. Gruff
  and lugubrious
always when I
  saw him
afterwards in his
  orchard, sucking
the wind-falls
  with his gums
he sweetened
  seldom. Yet
years later
  from a hospital
bed, bad coloured
  and dying, he

grinned at my
   crewcut, scoffing
at my father's
   derision. As I
preened his laugh
   redoubled through the
ward. One big grand
   fatherly hand burst
from the sheets
   to tousle my quickly
withdrawing head.

The Opium Smoker

Under his small
nostrils the
powder burns.

He heaves
and snores, his
ribcage rising

to enclose it.
On the
window the hot

sun whitens
like a coal.
Squeezed from

his lips
a frayed grey
plume drifts

in it.
As they tremble
above his

trunk's thin
folds of
skin, his rattling

throat, the
incubus passes,
blown through

a small ring,
a tightening circle
of silence.

Old Amahs

At corners on
winter mornings, the
amahs come out

for *haw fun.
Their eyes are
full of summer

evenings. Their min-laps
are buttoned tight.
In their pockets

the tram-car tickets
are faded and
curled up. Lodged

there since summer
the balls of
camphor have melted

away. Moths have
ravaged the sleeves
and linings, entering

them like explosions
leaving white puffs
of cotton behind.

*(A type of noodle sold by street vendors)

Girl with Bound Feet

She writhes
her toes pushed
down into her

sole, and strapped.
Her eyes, for a
moment, linger there.

As on some
faded vanity
she no longer

recognises. Behind
her a broken
wind chime

in a breeze
through bamboo
clatters. She sighs.

Gold in mud.
Storm wrecked blooms
under the dark arch

she walks through.
And always, now,
in evening air, as

the foot's unstrapped,
that jangling chime
through bamboo.

To My Blind Student Reading

   You move
your hand over
     a frost of

   paper, and
touch the
     papuled letters.

   They rise below
your fingers, and
     slowly mouth themselves.

   Their pressed out
meanings, where
     your eyes

   can't go,
are glimmered in
     the fall of words

   that slowly, softly
in your mind
     are settling

   like fresh
foot prints
     over the snow.

A Summing Up

You have sifted
and dreamed
the years

into a version
of words.
Everything expended

for this. You
think it is all –
your life

mine, theirs –
part of a
conspiracy of words.

They dream
us. From them
there is no remission.
.

The Stillness of Gardens

(1994)

First Frost

    This morning
a lighter
    light than light itself
like sea/horizon.
    Behind curtains
it waits.
    Stillness
of mineral, opaque
    silence. As if,
in this hush
    of air, the elements
are encouraging us
    to write
on the blank pages
    of our lives
again, the names –
    of morning, of light:
how to pronounce
    upon our tongues
that fragile
    white intensity
of their touch,
    their shape
as the eye perceives
    it leaning out to
wards what is not
    the mind only but
light, morning
    the first frost.

House of Birth

The stillness of the air outside
the window. On a January
morning. Far smudge of river.
A bicycle bell tinkling. Up
the pathway someone came.
Lifting your frosty
latch to receive him.
Dusting your step for him.
The breath which broke across
your frigid window; the scuttering
of tiny birds that lived
in your roof. Announcing arrival.
The water butt beside the wall
gurgled. Inside, the fire
flickered, but did not go out.
A foghorn blared far off on the river.

Corringham

Soft gurgle of water under my tongue.
The warm latch in my palm
opens. Here is a name
I can't pronounce. A tall tree
burns in its shadow. A house
of shutters, of diffused fragrance,
stands back from the road.
In the silence of its corners, under
its stairs, in cupboards, there is
a rush of air. Inwards, the field
breathes, inwards. A dark flame
topples towards me. In its bed
of fronds, the deep garden exhales
the secret of glass, of windows

The Listener

For you who are listening.
The locked cupboard in the wall.
The dust behind the wireless
on the floor where you sit,
amassing its silence. Valve glow.
Cursor streaming through light
of all those far away places. Names,
names, enveloped in static, words
across dark spaces. Outside
the snow falling, in the empty garden.
The gate squealing on its hinges.
It is you. Through all the years
drifting, you come back to greet me.
This small echo I hold in the ear
of the world, cupped intransigence,
the voice of a child, talking to itself
in a room of shadows; valve
glow, warmth of materials – wood,
glass, metal – a transcending
odour, drawing me near
to that conversation that does not end,
to that dark flower, that glass of
imperishable water, from which I drink.

Invasions

Brick dust. Cry of the curlew
over an abandoned field. Unaspirated
names of villages on the tongues
of new arrivals, down quiet
lanes. Along the river's bank
the crunch of grit on driveway
after driveway. Fierce push
of city families, above hedgerow
after hedgerow of acreages that
vanish. I stand listening
beside the wreckage of a coppice. Elm
and beech, falling, falling
through a stillness which could not last.

Then strange voices move, again,
up from the river, through dark trees,
felling words as they come.
Sceanc, giving way to *Leggr*.
Through ravaged vales. From
behind charred barns and sacristies.
A slow twilight seeps over saltmarsh,
pan. Within the breath of
drying channels, whisper of
unredeemable names. On
the air, rising and falling
places, things. Rising, falling.

The Chase, Corringham

The chapel floats
on its cupola of stone.
A slow,
episcopalian chant
beneath the ornate rose
window,
opening,
notes suete
onto the air.
Dogwood
rampant
beside the stile,
burdock.

Embedded in the wall
from the first chapel's
cope of stone
a hoof's half-moon
(buck or doe)
glitters.
In fading light
it's incised.
A deep scar.
In shadows
the scent of blood
dere to the dale
the ash tip thrust
under the heart.

High, under the eaves,
the melisma trembles
al the wode ryngeth.
Through the foliated dark,

                where hooves
                 of a distant
               long lost morning
                  thundered
              and were enclosed,
               the scent of wolf
                  of a rose
            moist snout snuffling
                   grasses,
                   lingers
                  stubborn
                is al myn song
              against silence.

The Visitor

One after another
they slid past
from quiet, lost sidings
where the trees reached
over the track and touched
deep green, twining
leaf and branch: *Cobham ..
Effingham .. Hinchley Gate.*
The silence rode
up their chiselled
consonants, and fell
onto the platforms.
After long years abroad
amidst fluidly
rising, dipping
tones of the Pearl
River estuary, he heard
for a moment
forgotten couplings,
*Brodshott .. Claybank ..
Stoke D'Abernon,*
collidings. Syllable
after syllable, laid
down upon the air.
And his tongue for
that moment, firm ties
taking the strain, silently
moved again under
an old familiar weight
and pull, amid broad
ploughlands, high-banked
lanes, villages in rain.

The Words

Where do they go to, loose
on the wind, itinerant small shadows
on this sunny day that has come
unexpectedly (the sun/the day)
carrying their message like small
change in the palm of the mind
as recompense for what they cannot
replace. We mourn, fluctuant
with no 'home', in their shadows
for that lost shape and density,
that exact history in which we breathe
and die. Here, hold out your hand
for them. Cup them. Feel
under the ragged pulse of their sound
the swift and turbid current bearing away
through the empty house, up the
deserted and defoliated lane, your time.
And, with it, that unconfirmed history
of who you are. That self un-named.

Scribe

Stone, drinks the moist wind.
The margin, too. Frayed
sloping cursive, all the way
to the edge of a slate
grey room. Knotty
frost cured fingers. The
serrated shadow on the wall
under the lamp, like a fossil
anchored in its glow, moves.
Across page and page
of unlettered silence the eye
follows it, with no punctuation.
Certain: certain of where it must go.

The Call

  Through a storm
of static, sand
  in air,
I hear at last
  your voice.
My ear pressed,
  for so long,
to the edge
  of silence, space
takes time
  to clear. Then
far off,
  behind you
the high, thin wail
  from a minaret
calls, through
  each filament of glass,
out of immense
  distances,
shifting endlessly
  between us,
all the faithful
  to prayer.

Meeting in Autumn

Like a fire died down and almost gone
out, the dulled gold of the leaves above
the water. The brimful depths are listening
to us as we stroll by, arm in arm, and talk
in leafy willow shadow. Scuffed at our feet the lip
of the bank of the canal. Meadow grass,
level and lustrous and lost
in that reflection that records upon itself
our own hesitant progression. The hour hand
laps the second hand in a sweep of fire. Sun,
amplitudinous on arms and hands and faces.
In the dry stone shade of a high wall
we stop, and kiss. Fragrance of leaf mould
on your cheeks, your hair, your lips.
Moss and fern above your head leaning
over to touch us, as I feel my pulse
your pulse, and hear under our feet the crack-
le of dead leaves, smell the thin plume of dust
as we move, rise into the air
to ignite, with your soft fingers and
your tongue, through all weathers here, our passing.

Waiting for My Father, 1939-45

Through all those long hot summer
afternoons
she turned the dial for news
amid a fury of static.
Or crouched in the dark earth
of the shelter.
Listening.
For words lost
in deepness of silence
unrelieved
by incendiary or explosion.
Be quiet   Listen!
Sound of footsteps
before the house.
The postman halted.
Then walked on.
Leaving the sound
only of a cricket
in tall grass.
It vibrated
across sun-blanched hedgerows.
The road, too, simmered
in its deep curve.
And waited.
In that silence
drifting through garden and rooms
she ground her fear
into a cold hard
irrepressible groan.
Edged it, at times,
with a sharp hiss.
Like gas
before it ignited.

Bonfire
(*i.m.* R.A.)

Silence drifts through your bones
like lead, dragging the smoke out
of the sky. Your eyes smart
as they stare into that flame
that ignites dried piles of leaves
dead stalks and twigs, the debris
of a summer. I catch you,
for an instant, as you turn
and squint, and try to hold
that look across the blurred
lines of all the years
that have passed. At the end
of a garden, now, someone is
raking and piling leaves. I listen –
for that false summer, mind begotten.
It crackles. It turns to a cinder.

Chinese Red Pine

Usurped presence,
obliterated silence
of boughs
that bend down
in summer's green
antiphonal and touch, words

are reparation
fragrant repositories, filling
with thing, or place
remembered,
not abandoned

within which
a shadow moves,
wind blowing
the ripe scent of it.

The shadow
of all dependencies
all departures,
in summer's green

antiphonal, touch
ing words
that are chimerical,
that can't be touched.

The Stroke
[D.B.A]

Darkness
of the
unworded, the unuttered.
Paralyzed sound.
Blood drowned
syllables. To go
out of the world
without a sign
in vocalis
to those close by.

As I gazed out
over the dark
March marsh
after her
the frigid white skeleton
of a tree
laid its leafless shadow
upon my tongue:
alder,
alnus glutinosa.

Air

vacant, mesmerized
rang
with the catena
of its sound.

Near Bridge of Allan

Red Ochils,
wind crumbling
their faces. Snow
piled high
on Sheriffmuir.
Sycamore quivering
in ruined
doorway. Out
over empty
hills, kestrel
and rook
above pike and
bayonet. Rusting
knots of iron
silently foliated.
Sill. Twisting
all the way to
the coast. Incarnadine
Ochil fault.

The Release

The heart's sweat of all those years
blows through ruined pages
only professed guilt makes her infamous.
The fierce rift of light
on margins. The invisible weight
of a marriage which ended.
I take it now, in the heat
of this mid-day shadow,
(in a waste-basket a torn up photograph of myself)
and wrap it in this sprig of tiger-grass
its dried breath-like edges, in this
sound of a cicada toiling at the centre
of its own life, and lift, and let
                        it
                                        go.

.

Window

As if it would extend for ever,
this frame of light through which
light moves. Opening.
Threshold. The tree,
sealed in it, burns. Within its silence
I hear hours steal
over the gaze of my reflection
– dark fluxion, lodged
within it. The air, too, leaning
inward, till there is nowhere
to go but here – this room,
table. Through the long
filtration of light upon the floor
the shadow of the tree draws back
through the quietness, slowly, of four walls
like a genuflection, to touch
my shadow, as they pass. As they pass.
Each with an unanswered question.

The Stillness of Gardens

We inhabit the stillness of gardens,
all our lives. Where the light
turns the pages of a silence
that listens. Where through
its slow dehiscence and exhortations
we try to touch, like touching a shadow,
a place we were born into but
outgrew. A quiet encirclement
of leafage sways in the margins;
a whisper, of warm showers;
a flickering light on walls. Imperfectly
remembered now, imperfectly
construed, they drift at evening
through our empty rooms.
We sit in the shadows, listening.
A bird sings, in the silence.
Like a latch opening within our
minds, a door entering into
a forgotten afternoon, its sound;
like the rustling leaf of a page
(smudged calligraphy, blossoming thumb)
we'll read and re-read the rest of our lives.

The Destruction of the Summer Palace, Beijing 1860

"In the Chinese garden the internal boundaries were made vague or ambiguous, time was made to stop and space became limitless ... it was a place apart ... free from the cares of men."
Maggie Keswick

After the conflagration of finials, a shout.
The *Rhus Vernificera* turned white.
A cambric sleeve melted in a hand.
The water in the moat dried to a dark stain.
Amid the heat and crackle of ebony galleries
the indigo of landscapes dripped and ran
down into the artificial lake.
All night they lay awake in their tents,
Coldstreams and Grenadiers, coughing
under the pall of a sooted moon.
In the charred ear of corn the reveille echoed,
and echoed. Through the wafted smoor
of rain they rose, their cloaks lichened with
damp ash. On their cheeks a dark stubble bristled.
Before them, insouciant imperial lions
glared from their singed plinths.

Lotus
(Chi Pai-Shih 1863–1957)

In your sleeves
the silence
of crickets

the small
clear spaces
where you lean

your head

to watch
the lotus bloom

How smoothed
and pliant
the air

there   You
have entered it
as you would enter
a small
sunlit room
hesitantly
on quiet feet

And you have
left it
as you found
it uncrumpled
made
out of the silence
that sings

without a line
or shadow
out of place
but proportionate to
what you observed

a small
chaste repository
a home
for the birds

A Mute, Inglorious Vegas
(For David O.)

Hot air. Night.
In the room
a smell
of ripe papaya.
He walked
through shadows
debris of luminescence.
It was close,
so close to him,
that breath of his
delusion that he touched
it and whispered
into the walls its name,
till they gave back
its votive scent.

Above squeal and scuffle
of rat filled ootero
he heard its voice
amidst the shadows
in the flickering room.
All hope, ambition gone.
The city burning
crackling
in its cerement of light.
Then placed some pesos
in the palm
of one beside him. Inhaling
on their breath
the scent
felicitous and dark

of papaya.

Indonesian Musicians at The World's Fair, Paris 1899

What rite that passage through innocent seas
would launch, what mud, what agony would accompany
its longing for older, far-off shores
where, from under the banana and
the mango tree, from under that steep
blue Balinesian sky, they beat
with a furious delicacy the air, the force
of their percussion caught in the ear
of Europe, as it sat and listened
and waited - waited, and waited, till it
knew that something was being abandoned.
A melody in fragments, unable to go home.
Dark pastoral. Cobblestone through a window.
All the bells in the belfries of each small town
tolling the fading Angelus. Outside, a crazed
wind in the trees, tearing up the score.

Émigrés

A small room, full of
light and birdsong and
stillness, we cannot step out-
side of. Here, we are our own
echoes. We metabolize
behind windows, all the dawns
of our past life flowing into
this space, all its successes
and failures. Journeying
homeward, we are lapped
by the shadows of an infinite
nostalgia: calls
on the air, from roads,
from bridges. They lead
nowhere. They pass through
us, like the lost rooms
and gardens of our childhood.
We stand here, and listen
to them. Heartbeat. Traffic.
Lost in stillness. Our feet have
wandered to another place. Already
our bodies are embraced by
its sly oblivion, its distance.

What's Left

Resonances at evening
of a still light, a garden
where the air is full
of fragrance, and shadows
rest easily, and are at
home. In borders, under
a wall: the dark earth
breathes. An insect crosses
the path. Punctuated progression.

Days write, on the journey
back, illegible annotations.
But there, half remembered
half forgotten, the gate's
left open for you to enter
worn out, with your bag
of artefacts and tokens.

Black Confetti

(1999)

Snow

Over the quietness of a far lane
and field, I know you are falling
through a debris of bones and cans,
unaware of how I pronounce the name
of what it is you are. Indifferent:
etiolated. From my cool lexicon
of air you are expelled, onto
a coloured earth that holds you.
As silent as the drift of smoke, of
light, of our secret selves. Fugitive.
You fall through my fingers
with a lightness of breath whose
only sound is a sound I cannot hear,
but imagine. I listen, patiently.
And, slowly, through the quiet shift
and slough of syllables, there is snow,
unexplained, unpronounced, falling
on gate and window. In my mouth
I have formed a silent O to catch it.

[Hong Kong, 1994.]

Post-Colonial Memorabilia

Like faded graffiti on walls, these names
of other streets, other roads: Old Bailey, Arbuthnot,
Blenheim. And this light that reflects
from the palm; slow, numismatic.
On the perforated postal order; on the embossed red
crown of the postbox; on the *On Her Majesty's
Service* envelope. The inauthentic dream departs,
taking with it a packing case of mementoes and
insignias, the sound of a leaking memory
of phrases infrequently used, poorly pronounced.
To resurrect, on the other side of the world,
what's 'lost', what's gone … another nostalgia.
Leaving, in its place, an afternoon
finally confirmed in its own right, on its own terms.
The signposts all pointing one way.
The roads and the promenades always
coming back in their sweep to this low
scorched promontory and, on smoke wreathed jetties,
fragrance of incense at makeshift shrines.

[Hong Kong 1996]

Holidays

Light trapped in a shutter;
hosanna of horizons. As we drift
up the last hill, idling
at the top, to silently gaze
on the anticipated immensity inside us.
Edge, falling off into a space
that is endless. High call
of the merganser. Air
of salt washed into our eyes.
A wave dreams against a head
land of crystal, somewhere
behind an embankment. No snapshot.
No souvenir. No memento. Adrift
on the deep insurgency of our shadows.
The restlessness of centuries ignites
quietly in the heat. In our bones.
The smoking hoof:
beat of migration. A rhythm that translates
through us into the light. Superscription
of years we cannot forget.
Shimmer of long, far off horizons.

Winter Monsoon

Crackle of surfaces, of dry air.
Dusty imbroglio. Contracting
and jolting the frames of windows,
stropping the humid warp
of paper. From far north,
across the sands of the Gobi,
gathering, for us, such limpid
pools of light. Our shadows drink
from them. Through the tombs
of the Ming emperors
it blows. Through corridors
of cold stone, touching our hands,
our coats. Soughed in the tilt
of grasses. Its thin, high note
a love cry through our rooms.
Altering invisible compasses.
Strengthening, slowly,
that irrepressible current in our veins.
Through the leaves of the cinnamon
and the pepper trees it rattles,
over the granite wharves beneath the hills
and the torn whitecaps on the bay.
As we lean into it, we breathe
the unmistakable aroma of capsicum;
the fierce fragrance of a dream,
its fine white powder ground
in a mortar, drawn through an alembic
of high wind and sea, of broken spars
and stunted masts, doldrums and calenture.
It hovers here, round these calm headlands.
Amid the stale residue of our lives, it is reefed.

Clearing Customs

After the drone of monotonous interrogations, to pass out
into the heat of exuberant foliage, lemonade stalls,
tin roofs under papayas. How can one 'declare' that
of which one is still so innocent. Reading the news in bed
in strange hotels beneath indigo mastheads of papers
thrust under the door. Scouring shelves of bookstores
for an inventory of shadows, a faded atlas annotated
by those who have passed here before. To dissect
loneliness fill in your name and address, on endless forms.
And observe the light, how, rising and descending on
your skin it enters a transparent country you have traversed,
but hardly know. The monstrous farrago
of its impedimenta overwhelms the senses. So we go
into this moist night full of objects inscribed with
our delusions. The indecipherable mystery of who we are.
And, from the strangeness of its fabrics, the unfamiliar
torsions of its smiles, we subtract ourselves, and the vanity
of our possessions. To leave – deracinated shoe, noctambulant
shadow – in the heat and dust of its fierce tableau, 'nothing'.

The Quay

Anchorless heart, out of flux of shadow, floating
on a white wave, as if entering an area uncharted.
In dull quay-water, flickering names. All the places
that summoned him! Names vouchsafing blandishment,
dalliance amid heat and dusty back-streets. Cities,
suburbs, suffused with light! Scent of guava and
frangipani. Odour of goat middens and grilled meats.
Incense of alterity. In innumerable smoke-filled bars,
nightly, listening to voices: imprecation and bravura,
in a language he did not understand. Whose speakers
understood his. In pensions, *VACANCIES* signs
bending and fading in fierce light, calculating leisurely
the weeks until expiry of visa, when he'd move on.
Cooled each night by on-shore breeze over mangrove,
he would etch on air destinations. Inventories of desire
his hands could touch. Or simply flotsam of boredom,
insomnia! Uncharted, untutored heart. Mind drifting, on
a sea which, he knew, would always take him back to
solicitude of quay and shore from where he'd come. One
from which he would, inevitably, again set out. Summoned.
By scented littorals. Chimaera. Impecunious isles.

Remedios Circle

"In the circle beginning and end are the same"
              Heracleitos *Fragments* (103)

On this hot night, in this circle of stone and worn grass,
by gates of dilapidated mansions, friends, families saunter
out from stifling shacks, children romp under streetlights,
vendors rest their carts on curbs. Behind glass
and hanging plants, in air conditioned draught, waiters yawn.
The end of day. Uncontaminated memories float
with the scent of the pomelo tree, over brick walls
and sluggish esteros. Over lichened stone angels,
over broken balustrades and marble fonts.
The leaves of the santol tree shine under the moon.
On the sidewalk a fretwork, flickering pattern; light
alternating with shadow, as cloud moves. We stroll down
a road that's quiet, unillumined. The dead gases of the city
hover above our heads. A jeepney stops by us. In it
the scuffed toe of someone's shoe traces an incomplete
circle, amid husks and scattered rinds, upon the floor.

The Garden

Beyond the crumbling statuary of cement,
flyover, pedestrian bridge, water tower,
behind the walls of a derelict dark garden
there is a pool of healing grey water, that glows.
Asphalt run-off, dew; impure elixir of the night
made clear again among contorted
petals, riot of shadow, where the twisted iron
of a gatepost knots the leafage of an almost
extinguished fragrance. Drink here, in the dust
of this silence, within the walls, from this
slowly gathered condensate. And savour, for one
moment, before you pass, what rises before you
in the dusk; familiar ghost, crepuscular face
of inarticulate longing, torn out of the earth
from such depth that even the chancrous stench
of the storm drain ebbs away before it.

On an Unnamed Avenue at Evening

Through the stutter and throb of traffic a note,
chord – heard/unheard – fading somewhere
beyond the lamp's glow, where your arm
is buried in shadow. Irrepressible rhythm,
syncopation, our lives make tracking us
through each day, hour, minute. You hear it.
In the evening. It's silent concatenation
on railing and step. The dark ripples against
you for a moment, washes through you
with it. You lean your head back, and inhale
the dank odour stirred by the fan, then walk
over to the window and lay your hands upon the sill.
An almost imperceptible movement runs through
them. Phantoms crowd round you. Memories,
desires, illusions. Then drift up, like smoke. You
stand at the window as it darkens. And listen.

To Every Window

Hot air, blowing through corridors, stairwells
and on landings. Odour of sweat and sampaguita.
The ephemeral music of bars. Through the gutted
heart of the Pension Casa Blanca charcoal drifts,
powdering the weeds in spectral yards.
Behind us itinerant musicians sing
beside the deserted underpasses of the city.
Night carries the weight of their song to every window.
God Is Love, in huge bold letters, stares from
a jeepney. A blue, electric light floats over
Ermita. In the shadows, rats. The sound of voices
that don't know whether to agree or contend.
Invisible lives. In the soft glaze of her eyes a liminal light.
Scraps of memory. Incomplete biography. We turn
into a dark alleyway. I press my cheek into the hollow
of her cheek. Nothing. Only, in her
austere smile, the inclement emptiness of the night.

Nightsong

Night's fragments caught in the eddy of air
from the open window; thin residue of diesel
from a parking lot, jigsaw of voices, odour of a
flower I cannot name. Dark heart beating beside me
to the throb of a generator behind the trees. In the sultry
air straining, manufacturing its dreams. The ambient
glow from a street light falls onto the floor. Through the
condensation on the mirror, half in shadow, I can
almost see her face, the gentle lineaments of mouth
and nose: that brief cartography of desire, where
the night is inscribed. From the house next door, the
strains of a lost childhood rehearsing itself on a piano
enter the window, and echo on out into the rest of the
Circle: and her hand grips tightly, in sleep, mine.

The Kiss

"You're afraid the kiss might betray you
  to other beds now of the past
  which nevertheless could haunt you."
        George Seferis

Now sleep has robbed her make up
of its lustrous glow. Upon
her pillowed head the night
breathes noisily. She does not stir.
In the unrobed dark of her skin he inhales
a shadowy crucible of old intimacies
a fragrance, an unexhumed sweetness
of journeys commenced, unforetold
destinations. Confused, he spends the night
looking for her. Amid the ruined
images of day he finds her, pensive,
sad, as if she had come back
to a room she needed to recompose,
imperfectly remembered. On her ankles
and feet a dusty, phosphorescent pallor,
as from wild untramped roads, lingers.
And doubt, scavenging her face
for something that is not there.

Remains

As if her hands were suspended in a gesture
of adoration: inscrutable shadows of her
being furled around her. He bends over her
body. Fragments. A last conversation.
Then silence. He follows clues. Trying to
elicit from her face the obscure
auguries of her heart. Hands
clasped in front of her: perhaps
in ritual scourging: or the simple
economics of predation? Either way
he knows her kind did not bury its dead
with flowers. And the dark bolus,
within the chest, she died of was not grief.
Shoes, neatly folded panties and socks
arranged beside her. Heart atrophied, puckered.
Suffused through it, like thickening cloud,
the long grey sediment of the life
through which she moved: her footprints,
preserved in it, echo. Yield only
a sieving of hints and whispers, an expired
dream, perhaps, amid a tumulus of shadows.

The Amanuensis

Through the obfuscated lines of his life
he walked. The darkness under his eyes like an ink
that had dried on a faded message.
Someone was there, in a narrow
room, in the clear light of his retinas, scribbling.
A treatise, on who he was. He heard
their faint sound, like a bird
scratching at a pane.
In a broken dream his hand
searched for a hand, and amidst the dream's
overlapping voices he heard his words
again, coming back to him
as if from the ghost of a life
through which he'd walked. Beside a courtyard
of dust and ragged palms, he paused, and listened.
Questioning who it was, who
made him speak through the enveloping night
on the unmarked street. And through yesterday's
rain he heard the long slow whistle
of the train as it was departing
for a country without names. And the sound of
his feet stumbling, again
and again, through the hot night, after it.

A House on Remedios Street

Where the gutter flows with a viscid white suspension,
through the long hot shadows of the evening.
Above steps, the oily penumbra of a lamp is thrown
outwards. A brackish emanation floats among the flower
pots, the ghostly breath of a dried out mangrove
in gardens, lingers, wet upon the arms, the
impress of a dying osculation. A streak of fragrance
where the hairpins dropped, is gathered now,
on the kerbside's quiet, where the cambered dark runs
into the trees, small airborne fires, *ignes fatui*,
hover. And small boys, following them, leaping
to cup that luminous particle in their hands.
Across the broken sidewalk, comes the rapid soft flutter
of a fan, followed by its shadow, and the long
inhaled breath of an ageing matrona at the top
of the steps, smoking a cigarette, lost in contemplation.

The Home of Pain

"In Rusafa I came upon a palm …
 I said: you stand alone, like me so far from home."
       Abd al-Rahman

The world goes on and on, transforming itself.
Memory sings day after day, excavating the secret
repositories of hope, despair. Over the road, Ospital ng
Maynila tops its drive of tattered palms, a thin stream
of antiseptic wafting through open wards out into
night-time traffic. The water in the bay lapping steps
arrives at the end of its long journey. Our dubieties rise,
multiply. In the crowded forecourt of the mind what
image is enjoined, to which they defer: whiter than
sheets, cooler than ice? Let us reach over and touch
it before day, choked with equivocations and lies,
dissolves it. Or is it only another tattered palm, tearing
in turbulent air, waving the soot of its striated shadow
before us; a dream, rooting and uprooting itself
in the rubble of a past it cannot remember, or forget; but
to which it is condemned, endlessly, to keep returning?

The Flight
(*in memoriam* N.V.M. Gonzalez)

Within this cooling swathe of light, the earth's unwrapped.
A rush of wind on a white wing.
Ascending, out of the path of something
hard and true, something immeasurably dense and rich,
into what? Beneath us, San Fernando glares
under a tropical noon, clearly laid out rooftops and walls, a grid
of streets transfixed; sharded light lifts up from them.
On one side, the sea's wrinkled integument,
brilliant strip of calcined sand; far out
umber of coral, water bruised to a deeper tint
of itself. On the other, as we tilt, following us,
narrating our journey, the high green of the Cordillera
lush in drifting cloud, pines gripping
in cold wind off each ridge, a silent geography
where water pours thousands of feet through air, without sound.
You look down, upon a road of moving palms.
A tricycle weaving through its cloud of dust.
A carinderia. A clump of banban. The land, spread out
beneath you. Caught there, in the stubborn terrain
of the senses, it had burned day after day, year after
year since you left, or did not leave; fashioning a voice
in which it might co-exist with that image of itself
you had taken with you, were impatient to reclaim.

Spring, the Return

Chatter of chemical codes among the trees. Language of
arrival, departure. Like migrating birds, names in the air. People,
places. Undeclared itineraries. Voices drifting over estuaries, roads
dusty with the feet of a procession under agoho trees.
Across stairwells fresh with the odour of jasmine after a death,
rooms stale with the air of connubial evenings. TV sets
left on all night. Messages unanswered. A door, closing.
And the mind always coming back, being's insomnia, to this
thin revenant of light upon the floor, pulse of the present and
the future, to the heart's incoherence, its unappeasable shadow.

In Time

The articulateness of roads. Recovering the sound of their speech.
Smooth as deceit, turbulent as terror. Their note a continuous
      reverberation
on which we are travelling, modulating from asphalt to earth,
leaving behind us, in the fumes of the noodle factory, in the frenzy
of the slaughterhouse and the dead river behind it, the smell
of time. Rising, with a clear tropical light, *liwanag ng araw*, on
their hard shoulder. We hear, in their monotony, the mileage
of our accelerated desires, the promiscuousness of boundaries.
We ride them, weightless for a moment, listening,
over bridges, beside water, to how we move from one
part of ourselves to another, questioning their sly camber,
the way the distance glimpsed at their centre is like the silence
of empty rooms, and the way the wind rustling their verges
throws into our voices a far away accent and pronunciation of
      longing
for what we will, we know, in time, grow tired of and discard.

Liwanag ng araw: *Tagalog for the brightness of day.*

City

The great stained boles of coconut trees on its flooded
sidewalks peel and fray. Their shadows macerate.
Unrestrained, infected waters seep into its river
where they bloom. In its markets at dawn
pale ubod roots are piled high in baskets
beside flyovers. Displaced families beg in the fumes
of traffic. Massive realty hoardings above the roads
advertise joys of country living – fresh air and views.
At the airport and wharves those emigrating
gaze sadly back. The track marks of the
last rebellion still visible on striated kerbs.
Dark and igneous, a volcano showers a fine ash
over rooftops. The voices of its women are beautiful
through long nights when the turbines of its generators
do not stir. In the ruins of their eyes streets
and alleyways are transformed into a maze of paths
that flower. Satellite dishes slowly rotate to receive
signals of earthly iniquity. In its bus stations
clouds from millions of journeys gather and are dispersed.

Mises-en-Scène

At the corner of Nakpil Street and Adriatico a boy
half trots balanced between two dripping translucent blocks
of ice, water that's still that flows between the arms
of embracing calipers. A warm, procreant wind gusts.
The downpour long over, the roofs of drying shacks
smoke like embers. At the intersection of del Pilar and Quirino
Avenue, oblivious to traffic, a child a-squat on the sidewalk
repeatedly decants from one paper cup into another
with a mesmerised look a stream of the clearest, pure water.
Like a bracelet around her ankle, a dark betrothal,
flies gather round a wound. And a taxi driver
approaching the end of his twenty four hour shift, his engine idling
in shadow down an alleyway near her, furtively draws the thin
white dust of shabu, as white as snow, into his nostrils.

Of Christmases Past

2 a.m. ... And the wind outside
is piling drifts. A white surplice
thrown over the hedgerow. A silence
at the edge of fields. Noiselessly
someone steals in, then out
of the bedroom. 3 am ... That white
electric glare, defying sleep
and darkness, lighting impatient
hands at gifts. Now, no one
steals in, and I have no room
to steal to. But, sometimes, when
suddenly awake at 3 am,
I stumble through an absolute
stillness, and glare of light
strangely luminescent, to reach
a room that is not there.
Banana and papaya trees loom outside.
The air is hot. I stand, for one
moment, in the immense darkness
beyond the window. High up,
the moon's grey sliver glistens.
Light pools at my feet
in the cold, hard mineral of reflection.

Another Country

Late afternoon sun gilds the sacristy of Malate Catholic Church.
Through the trees sash and surplice drift, against
the gleam of polished pews. The heavy gold doors of the
Grand Boulevard Hotel slowly revolve. Aromatic day.
Huge, explosive encrustations of frangipani sweeten
the air. The fragrance of sesame cakes, from a vendor,
floats. Beside the road, their feet stirring the rubble
of the sidewalk, three girls perch on a narrow wooden trestle.
Bar-whitened faces, dead-end downturned looks. Their eyes move
from side to side, up and down, then out over to the sere grass
of Remedios Park, where a glittering wave on the bay
unloads its light. Behind them, in the sanitized glare of
Dunkin' Donuts, tourists eat. They wait. The damp
wind of a dusk begins to linger in their hair. The fumes of jeepneys
stalled on Mabini invest their clothes. A bride and groom rehearse
through the trees, their fateful walk. Flicker of gold on the finger.
A young tourist with a half eaten doughnut in his hand
comes out, and begins to talk. 'Paraiso, parang ibang bayan.'

Paradise is another country: a Tagalog saying

Lux in Domino

                        Beside the railway tracks a black
frocked priest says Mass, washing the feet of the unabsolved.
On the fronds of coconut palms the spindled light is threshed
into a fire. Moving through space, through time,
the unargued premises of our lives persist. Ascending
carpeted stairs beside alcoves where little mock Roman porcelain
love-gods smile. Breathing the smell of far-off rain. Behind
high walls of compounds the sonorous voices of children fly,
birds out of foliage. Lines, from the epithalamium of a discarded past,
return. In the shadow of a broken hand pump water spells its name.
The cracked earth draws in its breath to listen. Over the rails
from the freight-cars comes the smell of condemned flesh. Livestock,
hoof deep in piss. Who will stand and say a prayer over them?

Maginhawa Street

The blighted face of a word. Noxious creek.
Dark estuary of lives, washed up. Prostitutes, shoelace
vendors, the occasionally employed. Through
the capital's sempiternal heat they drift, linger, lean against
each other, and then are gone—into another sodden labyrinth
of muddy alleyways, with roofs held on by rocks and
tyres. Here, in this room's cramped shadows, wafts
from under the door an odour of rice-cakes and effluence.
Someone, groaning, stirs at the end of the afternoon
released from a haunting dream of beer or shabu,
and curses. Their ruined discourse drifts by us
on the floor. I feel the warmth of your small waist
in my hands. Emaciated kittens scavenge outside
amid the debris of rotting eggshells and bones.
Old men sleep behind grilles in *sari-saris* their heads abuzz with flies:
on shelves behind them the labels on canned fish have curled
and faded in fierce light. Tethered by a length
of string to its leg, a chicken attempts to fly.
Your mouth opens and, in its darkening flesh, glows.
Like stars, your fillings give back the last of the remaining light.

Maginhawa: Tagalog for comfortable

The Stair

You have always been in all of my poems, a secret
odour, an atmosphere, pervading their sound;
of open wounds, of roads going off into sheer light.
In the deepest vicissitudes of their syllables you have promised,
as you pronounced them, pain and joy, trailing behind you,
in room after room, a fragrant pharmacopoeia
of sighs. Dark door of alterity,
the pores of my words open to receive you. You,
who come from far off with the dust of a long journey
on your heels, the expression of indigo skies in your smile.
You watch the wind drive the rain into the eyes
of the sweepstakes ticket buyers on Leon Guinto as if
they are tears, and look at me out
of a lopsided shack of plywood and tin, a dim alleyway
awash with offal and water. Your eyes are alive
with the vocabulary of the living, the dead, and those not yet
born. I carry your dark gaze within me,
an acid eating my flesh, a shard gnawing
my shadow, through streets where poems are written on the façades
of buildings, in brick and dust, and where, in a whitewashed wall,
a thin stone stair climbs perpendicular and,
twisting like a waist near the top, suddenly goes out of view.

The Lovely Cow Dung Flower
(So Nam *1944-94*)

Hurled to the ground,
where you had slipped, or willed
yourself through that open mouth
of appetent air, at, almost
the precise moment of the year's
turning, leaving behind you
son and wife. As I leaf
through your poems now,
our photograph beside
me – a finger from my own
failed marriage tensed
above the shutter – you reinvoke
in the lost fields of Kamtin
your childhood, and you remember
your lost love, your
"life long ambition [so] cruelly
forsaken" – "Suzie, of Morrison
Library at Berkeley, Sun Shine land
Garden of Love." And I wonder
if in this little hill garden
in Yuen Long that you came back
to occupy, you could ever
forget that "radiant Beauty,
unsurpassed Sweetness," slipping
further and further from you.
Love; a continuance,
and an inconvenience, something
to look backward to,
like the lovely cow dung flower
that roots up through
your words, saturated with
the light of those bright fields

of Kamtin, to whose immeasurable
stillness and fullness
you would return, to regain
your lost poise; regained,
and lost a second time! Your unfulfilled
shadow slopes across this page
and I can hear your voice
again in my ear, whispering,
one week out of the asylum, afraid
of your wife. "Please remember
this endearing and enduring
name." Poet to poet,
Tu Fu dreaming of Li Po, I
send these words across that
"overwhelming chasm" to search
for you. "Soul mates for life,"
how could you not hear?

(The quotations are from a translation of Tu Fu's poem 'Dreaming of Li Po' completed by So Nam just before he died, and from the long dedication to Suzie which he appended to it.)

The Past

Shadow of harebell, flax
   waving, down those long
deserted lanes. In fierce
   September light I hear
them, in the wind, moving:
   rustle of down,
stalk. Buried in blossom
   the mind, pale simulacrum
of words; breathing through
   time, a broken calendar
of days. I turn, again, the page
   on a writing the colour
of light. Too thin, transparent
   to give back anything but
the weight of itself: soot
   of an extinguished flame.

Orchard Bungalow

Stays in the mind, its edges framed
   with high banked cloud, sunlight
on wall, trellis.
   Sound of birdsong, filtering
with light through hessian flap
   nailed on the frame of an outhouse
door. Faded, I can hear its
   scratchy finale still, its motif
broadcast over lawns and borders.
   Inside, all is stillness.
The antimacassars whiten.
   The roses, entwined
above the piano, open. Their scent
   a token, a promise, offering
to remain when they have gone.
   No shadow moves through
those sunlit rooms, disturbing
   the dust on settle and skirting.
In bowls on sills, fruit ripens.
   Like mind, slowly fermenting round
an object, an absence: as round
   the notes of some forgotten music.

Crepuscular Summer

If you listen hard enough
   you can hear, through the dry
crepuscular sounds of summer, the dead
   butterflies circle in air,
the shadows of a thin
   exhalation. And, under
your hand, rustling the edge
   of sunlight and water,
someone carving your name, on an
   afternoon you cannot quite remember.
Obliterated whole. Letters strung
   together from silence. The broken wall
at the end of a garden,
   the rusting latch of a gate,
the melody half heard
   through an open window;
neither imagined, nor real. Fragments
   you inhale on the desiccated
sward of the years, blown
   back and forwards. A leaking
arcanum. There, amid the smell
   of dead leaves and branches –
the water in a pool
   whose dark skin you break.
It still holds your reflection.

At the 26th University of the Philippines' National Writers' Workshop, Baguio

As if words could recover this light that spills
through the cones of the pine trees.
There is nothing that is so faithful, in the act
of being perceived, that we can record it
with any certainty. Even desire
moves, and fades. And the branches that bend
in the wind make no concession to this
glad virtuosity that threads through everything.
Like anonymous gifts, birds fly in the windows.
The approximate measure of our perceptions falls
before us. A thin light ripples.
                    Our minds are steeped in symbols.

Outside, late afternoon rain beats on concrete
and pine needles. In the wind that blows
through the room, following the birds,
the awkward grammar of a world, its predication,
slowly unfolds on the pages before us.
Texture of tongue, of breath. The unanticipated clause.
Like music, like music, the unrecuperable
sounds of the birds, far off, higher
and higher on the mountain, outrunning the storm.

Uncollected

(2000-2001)

from The Fragrant Emporia

Because of the hurried and unending train of his discourse I was not able to reliably identify the names of the places in which he had stayed. Discomposed by the intensity of his gaze I looked at his shadow, suffused with the odour of Gitanes, and listened. "Time never stops. From within time how do we know anything, except what is provisional. Each letter longing to unite with a word, each word with a sentence, and that sentence – a miracle! – to stand, finally, on its own."

......

Lost in the backward pull of what we have left; memories, possessions — death's shadow over us. They are siren voices. The black swell under the bright froth of the wave that sucks us down into an antechamber of stale echoes in which we will search for something that is not there. On the flight back a Lebanese merchant, a textile manufacturer from Beirut, who had studied in his country, looked into his eyes and said: "I don't think that after having lived in this continent for so many years you will be able ever to live again in your own country."

...   ...

In the silence of hotel lobbies you can still hear them, he remarked sadly, travelling through time, their unobliterated footsteps on marble laid down millions of years ago, their travelling bags dark with the hiatus of enquiries, their deodorized shadows caught in the glass walls of atriums like fleeting forms trapped in amber. Tedious merchants of conversations, carrying, somewhere deep within themselves, the chemistry of ancient atmospheres, of uninscribed horizons, their pink chins dappled with light refracted through thousands of identical rooms.

.

The inebriated instruments of the indigenous musicians at a pension of lice and shadows. Dung in the alleyways. A subservient populace. Escape into sound! He inhaled the asbestos of burned down factories. Sirens of police raiding down side streets, looking, in a ruined economy, to supplement their official pittances. All night a litany of drinks filled his glass. In the mornings they sought him out with a pornography of tears and he dozed, sometimes, unknown to them, in the dark while the projector flared. In the evening the toil of fragrant arms. By a harbour of stinking refuse the light burned to a deep pulsating blue. Avenues of sauntering bodies under the sagging power lines. The dust of white, mahogany shaded, village roads at dusk. And, somewhere, that elusive, and slightly shy, crepuscular smile of a youth. A wild mouth cupped in the dark, full of the sweetness of an uncorrupted source.

……

There was only sadness left in the arcades of desire. The statues' taut pressure lines of skin over muscle and bone were elaborated in the smile, or gravitas, of the statuary of the living. One night as he came back across the river, counting the bridges all the way down the dark, weed choked, estuary, he thought that the tide had left without him. Swarms of white ants, in the humid tropical night, flocked against the windscreen shedding their wings, and wriggling away. As the car stopped and he opened the door, he realised that it was a dream, and that no ship was waiting for him … They do not constitute us, the objects of our waking and unwaking, he thought.

.

You can go only so far, and then you can go no further. Wielding titles and diplomas in empty places. Scanning the horizon for another area to annex, or explore. The seas come up to you and wet the sky blue of your garment. What else is there to do, but disappear. Folded in the purest air of the invariant, the intervals of grasses and of books. The noise of wars. The sounds of amorous advances. In the half light he read the score of a child's music that was fading in and out of each refuge where he had sought some solace from a life of failure. Among the spines of gilded libraries. Among all conceptualizations. And, in his mouth he ran his tongue around, instead of words, the perfect and bitter roundness, the oblation, of silence.

Between

Plate glass
harbour, reflecting
itself;
meteorological beacon,
observatory.

Contours
vibrate to a sound
of theodolites
incising shape
between windy headlands.

Divisoria drowns
in a fume of gusts,
lacquered grime;
not
in one place
at one time
do we hear ourselves

fully, talking,
thinking, writing
one hand
pressed against
the shadows
of a city, moving

between
sudden alacrity
of grief
and an idea,
through time

dividing
and conjoining. Foliate
desire.
Light filling
the drawing rooms
of the planet,

railway terminuses
with enormous clocks
and, admist
discord of telephones,
the looks of abandoned
hope,

waiting. Limpid
conservatories of childhood
rift beneath us –
upholstered
dreams! The edge
the edge of something

beautiful
we heard,
in a room
or on a beach, its sound

leaving us breathless.
Always at all points
of departure
distance

viaducts, empty fields.
If only,
on the pale parchment
of the hour,
under the streetlight,
we could refract
through pure sounds
the news

of our arrival.
Trembling, with all we know
but cannot name,
indigo ink
of nights drawn down upon us,
looking up

only a tutelage of signs
to ferry us through
the dark matrix
of our selves to what
constructed place,
that could welcome us,
would we come
determinate, and brief
held by
              no other possessions
than these.

Belonging

(2009)

Light Where There Is

A figment
the whole drift
and slew

of air
fricatives colliding
in an empty place

leaves surrender
careless effigies
of who we are

and insistent
light where there is
dark undergrowth

grown daily
more rank
within extremities

of pain   But –
the air unheard
nonchalance pervading

itself and us
caught in the bend
of a wrist

transcribed
topography of sound
giving back what

we never were
can be
The grey face

in a rain of weeks
life dissolving
marls and toxins

And   as if
acacias were bent
shadows from the brim

of some immense
caprice a voice
a silence   It is

more than we deserve
knowing ourselves
so sparely to enun

ciate   So clear
Tides of a factory
scum foul odour

of regret for
things done not
done Yet

there is
joy simply
in the holding of

words on a page
that do not deliver us
from our selves.

A Habitation

The snowdrops, broken necked on tall stems under the trees have gone. Terracotta sun plaques line the sandstone walls of the courtyard. A curlew falls above a far off meadow. Where do the clouds go, but to the edge of the horizon. We are orphaned almost as soon as we can talk from the wind that leaves no names inside us. The river, a harried sound now over the earth's shoulder, echoes through the panes of the empty summerhouse and beside the drained swimming pool. Each day the sensations of our past come back to haunt us. Broken laughter at the top of steps, a particular look, smell, the angle of light across a face or sward of grass. They hover on the desks at which we sit poring over our dictionaries, catalogues and compendiums, the conduits of a place which we construct. Beyond the sound of all the words is the sound of the air, breathing. An empty road on the brow of a hill defines the limits of our field of vision. Maybe, though, if we were to utter our names again in the wind it would come back without them – having gathered, from these worn out and debilitated siftings, the source of all the names; that deep vacancy and stillness towards which each day the mind, along with the tired echo from the empty summerhouse, bends. And from which the swimming pool drains a slow fosse of light which ripples at the edge, as if it was filling.

The Pear Tree

Irresolute border, the wind shifting in
the hedgerow. Immaculate white lawn of
snow. Pale light moving across the river.

Where a face turned behind a curtain,
refulgent in shadow. Was it the curve of
the mind – the breath's camber – or a real figure.

For daylight's first loss, recorded nothing
but this. Beyond an open window night,
an immeasurable sadness of streets,
filling the intervals of a life.

Glow on buildings, railroads clanking in
the dawn's stillness, the smell of livestock.

And nothing differs, except the difference
of loss and gain. A memory of distinct
horizons and spaces, peopled by a question.

Rockpools. Calendulas in churches.
Tracing a likeness out of despair.

The pear tree filtering – like a great web of
suspended motes – air: looking up into it.

Would solve nothing, landscape, dream
figure that a mind makes, shifting
between itself and that imagined other.

Desire reduced to a brisk metaphor of exchange,
consumed, burned by its own transport.
Damp bodies, gathering sand on the world's littoral.

What we proceed towards
through the night's humidity day's rancour, tinkle
of goat bells across a far river bloom
of white dust upon dead words.

My darkling syllable strung upon a high
cloister, echo I listen for, faded angelus,
fingertap upon my broken window.

Turns, turns the light on in each dark
corner, "In the softly luminous hour tell
me a story, where nothing is more than
itself, an object turning in its own memory."

Is only this: an ember of dusk, caught in
the wind; a shadow that calls to us out
of an aperture in a garden wall, from another country.

Edges

Body that has no country
no map, no horizon to navigate by.
It sets out on,
and is the sole author of,
its own journey.
Unannounced, always
unexpectedly taking off into the blue of elsewhere;
bowsprit, the ideal music
of the purest memories
that have been ground down
into disconsolate atmospheres
in which we are waiting, breathing
the air of some where else.

In the reinstated constituents
of time and space, standing
outside a bookstore, the *Solidaridad*
on Padre Faura, thinking
what is the light doing
looking for a place
in which it could belong, watching
the dust turn ceaselessly
under the acacia trees.

Impermanent blue
shadow,
the treacherous edge
of a 'here'.
The wisp of a wind

would blow it away,
into a sky woven with
promises. It follows us
with the shape of leaking horizons,
the grey impersonations of waves
       that break upon
rooms filled with the saddest
of roses, of old photographs,
a haunting chemistry that blows
from some remote topography:
                        sounds
through an open window
that no one has heard before
or composed.

Place of unconnected moments
of infinite arrivals and farewells,
of a sail on a shore.
Whose is this face that we seem to remember
but can't quite recall:
the discarded fragment of a dream,
perhaps, a melody, intended to lead us
back to where it began.
Half heard conversations.
Unrecuperable names.
They shelve away down
to a broad sunlit avenue,
to trees that ripple
on a white plain
where lightning lacerates a dark sky.

In the stillness of 'not moving'
someone,
suddenly, thinks *home*.
Dark petals
on a sill, a lace
curtain bending in,
corroborate, and mock,
    a sense of being
somewhere else.

Ideal place of memories:
                  glimpsed –
        then gone.

Lisping,
sometimes, in the coordinates
of a lost tongue
it brings back to us
              nothing
but the kapoc tree at night in bloom
and the shadow of the one
who passed under it,
at noon, muttering
who am I, carving
his signature out of the wind.

A Boyhood

Not a sound
through the dark
air only
a dog barking
click of a dynamo
on spokes, before sleeping

house fronts.
Cold latches.
Environs, barred
to him. Days
held in the element
of despair, floated

up a hill
past the wooded
moat of sky. To
where, and who,
beyond himself,
was watching, if at all

the land forming
round a question,
river moving
through its treacherous sediments,
Shoreditch, Purfleet, Gravesend,
while the marsh burned

white flesh from stalks
and the church threw
its pointed shadow across the vigour of
a dead pastoral. Ominous
succession of signs; words

to denigrate
the shape of the tongue, stuttering
father's employment, school.
Supineness before authority.
'The best infantry in the world.'
He heard

the afternoon sigh
on the ragged verges
of council estates,
where the shop fronts creaked out of their
broken names and hoardings

'Alston, Edwards, Nunn,'
generations that stayed,
and the light, pouring
through orchards and graveyards,
and birdsong. Journeys, beginning

and ending,
a twilight
of narratives. Where
the river moved
amid the summer spores,
nettles and dockleaves

through small creeks,
trickled, he wrote
his name
upon the softened stump
of a rotting aspen
branch, and launched it.

Belonging

    To no where
to no thing
to the shortest abridgement
of air   of word
to   the cruel insignia
         of our acquisitions.

Lost
under damp swamp of cloud
     muddy field
          the moon
's light
        very first embrace.
Still missing.

The scent of what lies
  at the end of the road;
     a copse
of guava trees, perhaps,
      or tamarind:
  suffused in the wind,
gathering   and dispersing.

   Flame
             in windless rain
that keeps   burning
          hand
of the one who doubts.
                    The sound
of a pure line of thought   running
    carrying over
             into the present.
Beside the table   a blue chair
    with all the confidence of
       a disclosure
leaning into space
    and silence.

To no particular
  time   or place
    then.
Under the shadow   of the rain trees
   I saw her hurrying
towards what
          was only
a distant speckle of light
  upon a   possible event.

                    Heard
      in the rustle of
that air,   as it was
                        departing,
another moment   arising.
            A history
of burned pages.

Cannot come back
      cannot, ever,
                  return to
      where it was,
                  crushed between
those pale linens
                        a sprig
of purple   sweetening
       the tongue.

            Was
the width of a breath
between us,   crossing
  the hot courtyard,
               unable to compose
ourselves   through all those
       annihilations
we had not spoken of
    over which we
had no control.

The dark saxifrages,
   in a crevice
on a slope,   bending
   in the breeze
of a bright morning
                having,
      unlike ourselves,
                     no need
   to locate
just where they are.

Move
      across
   this sandstone wall
      this acropolis of air
your voice
         so that the emptiness may spall
               and stain
      into it.

      For
what we are
            excluded from,
      the roots' white
            intricate knot,
                  air
through the thin shadows of our bodies
            refutes,
         grinding the rocks
under our feet   dissolving
the black ashes of words
      in our throats.

Signifies only
    what it does not
        possess
but will go on   looking
    for
among all the vagaries and evaporites
    that attend it
                leaving
in this trackless dust
    a footprint,
        the pale ghost
of a voice
            crossing a road.

Archipelago Nights

Bone white sheen,
and she has slipped
quietly away
from you in sleep,
the phosphorescence
of a shallow lingers
wide, enveloping
arm, leg

                         antiphon
of doomed corals,
a submerged republic
that rides up onto
the waters of the night,
bring back voices
over the surf, into
this quiet

                         who
shuffling back, late
from that shore
of lost spirits,
wasted no time
in enfolding, street
by street, an entire
imago, the chaos
of your life, in her mind

                         a skull
of forsaken memories,
emporia of dreams, where

remains of the displaced
and the exploited grip
the eyes' ebb, flight
towards another coast
that's unenveigled, transparent

                    gauging
the precise angle
of the head and feet, the
body's disposition, waits
among the abaca and
the looms of shipwrecked
hands, and dances,
though the signs
are not propitious

                    speaks
out of the dried up
reservoirs, the slums
of bought-off voters, declining
to name the price
of silence, her hands
arranging the wreathes
of victims, spread
and undressed

                  binds,
with a calla lily,
the broken waist
of the water,
a bracelet of tiny scars
round her wrist,

the blood of indentured labourers
on haciendas
darkening her streams

                          drawn
into each small
hollow, cove, breathing
an exile's prayer, an anthem
of deception,
the filth of clogged esteros
filling the streets,
you wait,
uneasily, on the night's
escarpment of bone

                where
flotsam, gulls,
and driftwood meet
the horizon, level
with the edge
of some glittering repose,
the heart pounds
solitary, moving
between itself and others,

                        clear
light of moon
to navigate you through
reefs, drawing
around you a fleet of ghosts,
words – *land reform,*
abolition of oligarchy –

tilling air
to see
what will grow
on shifting current.

                    Thin
like a wafer,
they dissolve
upon the tongue …
indigent's breath,
crepuscular
flower of the retreating
jungle, invoking them
you invoke yourself,
again

amidst a catafalque
of blooms, of horns.
In desolate barrios, bound for foreign
aquariums, the doomed
corals of the republic
raise, like bleached bone,
their branches up
into an air in which
they drown.

City of a Thousand Lamaseries

Entering the city from the south, amidst heavy trundling carts full of a fragrant harvest of rice, and crossing a humpbacked bridge spanning the canal, if you listen carefully as you turn from one of the labyrinth of streets into another you'll gradually cease to hear what is happening around you – a peculiarity of this city of pilgrims – and start to identify the sound of your own breathing. In such an ancient topography of sound, passing citadels and shrines of all the various tutelary spirits who have at one time or another inhabited and been worshipped in squares and places your passing shadow brushes against, you will sense not only the dark of your own respiration but 'gates' through which the fluxion of so many prayers of previous generations of devotees and exiles before you have entered. Indeed, you will begin to feel, walking up and down these streets, that your own physiology is the site of a continuous liturgy, a repetition whose rhythm, if you could only manage to succeed in falling into step with it, would end, ultimately, in the act of your disappearance. Repeating the syllables of street names which seem almost vicariously to keep re-entering your mind you will begin to lose sense of any distinct direction in which you might be headed, and in your increasingly insistent circumambulations, over a ground which appears to be homologised with a transcendent plane, you will sense, if nothing else, your regressive structure of movement, syllable and word drifting on a current of air where the familiar ghosts of sounds are indelibly impressed. Each street you walk up and down will come to seem the same, whichever end you approach it from. Likewise the letters of their names, when repeated, eventually, robbed of the authority of the power of designation, will seem not to suggest difference so much as interstices in your breathing, holding within themselves a variance which is at the same time in agreement with itself – reversed, they would make just as much 'sense'. What are these words, then, you will ask, and the objects they denote, but portals through which, if you could pass freely from the chaos and longing of your own life, would open onto nothing except empty space. A space in which there would be nothing: no temple, no courtyard, no stream of incense from the moon shaped door and dark inner calm of the apothecary. Nothing. Only, within the memory of that self you could not deliver yourself from, and in the darkness of light and the endless interfusing of morning into night, a long strained for, and sought after, erasure

Flume

Rippled

tongue adrift
on shadows,
        pulled through
a world impatient
to sound

ledger
     of gleanings
anatomisings,
night's thin loams
   growing
whiter   towards dawn,
names of the lost

   particulars
air   with all its
lacrimations
      distractions,

listening
to what breaks
across itself
   colliding
with its reflection,
   syllable
               calling

back what
years discard,
    until you cannot hear
anymore
what it is they are

saying,
  cognate of
  to arrive
at a point
   cress pulled
   through clear waters
where one is
always

      departing
 forehead pressed
against
     wainscot
where you write
the names
      and listen:
they never
come back.

The freight
  of 'here'
       lilacs
weaving
beyond shadows
       one white flake
earthwards

                    where
in a river
of elided moments

   are you
as year ends,
under a token
of thunder
then
                silence
reconfirming

   what is
is at variance
   with itself
   syllable
                    calling

in wind
      the flowers
of the talahib
      kakawati

endlessly stream.

Interlocutors of Paradise

(2012)

The *English* Boat

"We are
Those Fractions of the Sum of Being, far
Dis-spent and foul disfigured, that once more
Strike for Admission at the Treasury Door".

Farrid ud-Din Attar *Bird Parliament*

Liquid Gold

In England under a grey suborned light many years ago, in air etched with bickering, birdsong 'ch-ee, ch-ee' *Turdus merula* : ornate variant of a rotundity expiring, through arboreal gloom, in a scratchy finale. Suddenly: like an indecipherable signature. Annotating a tract in which we had all conspired. Whose ink the centuries have dilated into this note. The past, in which we are all remembered without being named, performing all the obeisances and making 'the right noises', warbled. A scribbled note to those who might pass this way through the wood again. A little gold in the margin. Sifted song.

Farewell to the Shade

These twits and twoos, on a night of frost and bare trees. These too will echo in the wood, when the wood is no more. Echo, moon rising above hedgerows, when the king is no more: when the great landed estates, gentry and freeholders, are no more. Six thousand mature oaks for a man-o-war. For that which exists, *Strix aluco*, in the mind only, apropos the heart. What we have wrested from arboreal carnage: the sound of a nation transcendent, its voice. Even a tree can be without existing.

Kaah-Kaah-Kaah

On churchyard oak and immemorial elm, *Corvus frugilegus*, a parliament of dark chattering. Under a pall of smoke Drogheda burns. A man winces in pain, implores mercy. Bludgeoned with his wooden prosthetic limb, he gets none. Thick roosting of shadows. Clusters of hawthorn blossom lining the August lanes shake in a thunderous roil of air. The carrion mouth of the moment opens upon "barbarous wretches" and their "corrupt customs … licentious swearers, and blasphemers, ravishers of women and murtherers of children". Res nullius. For a form of government and polity that brought "England … to the height of perfection and happiness". For a land "adorned with goodly woods even fit for building … ships … as if that some Princes in the world had them they would soon hope to be lords of all the seas". A "lande so fertile as wanteth nothinge" – four fifths of it manhandled from its rightful owners. High in their cold colony, Corvus frugilegus, pitched into the wind, descend above the outstretched shadow of a man.

'To Get the Pearl and Gold'

Over salty shallows the scent of jasmine and tobacco flower drifted. In unworked mines. In deep woods of oak "farre greater and better than in England" revenue for settlement. Timber for ships for a country almost depleted of it. El Dorado. Subtropical air. Wading warm waters. Oyster shell middens on the shore. Shad, sturgeon and turtle. Bear and elk. Sumpweed and marsh elder. Gourds, beans and squash. "Let cannons roar … Go, and subdue". A continent for their taking. All, one day, the detritus of Europe. Tearing "a more kinde and loving people …, not [to] be found … void of all guile and treason". 'Tearing' they came < from the Latin *vulturus*. To 'purify', as they might have said, the savagery of their heathenish ways < from the generic *Cathartes*. So as the sun went down above the hills of Roanoke Island, *Cathartes aura*, nostrils perforate and lacking a syrinx, grunted and hissed from a dead tree defecating on its legs to dissipate heat. Was that not a voice prophetic of what was to succeed it – appetency and fear? Grunted, and hissed. Contrasting, or not entirely, with that sweetly anointed tongue: "only my father would keep such a bird in a cage"? Journeying from Munster estates of forfeited land across the sea to her – "the Ladie of the sea". Composing an encomium. Accompanied by another who sang, also, sweetly to her. His song, upon that "interminable waterway" that reached to the farthest ends of the earth, running softly in his companion's ear.

Out in the Open

Among the whitethorn hedges, beds of burdock and nettle. On the lichened tree trunks light, a golden wash. Scent of hellebore and vetch. Small ploughed fields fenced in where once there would run to the horizon common and meadow pasture, manorial wastes, marsh. Song of *Turdus merula, Turdus viscivorus* usurping that of *Vanellus vanellus, Numencus minutus, Perdix perdix*. From exiled song retain, on the wind, crunch of grubbed up livelihood of centuries fed to the sheep's gut, silence of grass growing in doorways and floors of abandoned houses, felling of wood and copse. And sound of a gentry chewing, growing fat on its appropriations of land increasing rapidly in value fifty fold. Cottagers and commoners deprived of acreage for grazing their cattle, sheep and geese, for berrying, gleaning, fetching fuel, hunting and cultivating; turned into paupers or, no longer independent, fodder for factories in cities. And, if they stubbornly resisted, hung, disembowelled and dismembered. From a parliament of landlords plush on its hassocks and rents, retain, too, the refrain " labour every day in the year ... put out [children] to labour early" so that the "subordination of the lower ranks of society ... would thereby be considerably secured". And then turn, again, to this neat arcadia of cottages and small fenced in fields with their hedgerows a foam of blossom – over them the ethereal anodynes of a popular imagination hover, the hoarse perorations of politicians held hostage by sybaritic noise, the importunings of investors, the unending inanities of celebrities and their besotted media – and inhale, deeply, the old lie of a bucolic idyl.

A Place Insufficiently Imagined

The astonished white wave broke and ran amidst red-fruited ketaki thickets; amidst "streets large and well paved, the Trade great … the Merchants rich, the Artificers excellent." But the master weaver craftsmen of Dhaka stood with bleeding hands, index fingers and thumbs severed, a generation of teachers – never such fine muslin (wrapped in 'air') lace, 1,800 threads to the inch, again woven. Obliterated. To protect and foster the growth of a garment weaving industry back home. And the land, grain reserves having been prohibited and many fields once sown with grain forcibly given over to indigo and cotton bound for overseas markets, exhausted, yielded famine. A third of the population dead. And profit. "There had been nothing like it since the Spanish Conquistadores looted the Aztec and Inca civilizations". And opium, spices and precious stones. "Enormous profit" stoked the furnaces of a Revolution, its "structural development" at "every possible level", back home. Ash-grey, deceiving bird, *Cuculus varius*, 'pipieeta … pipieeta' endlessly amidst the ketaki trees, using an other's nest, lining its own.

Through starching heat, through blood red leaves of fire trees and silent fierce-white compounds at noon comes, up the long shaded corridor of the close, that note again.

Customs / Duties

At the customs house at the Ch'ung-wen Gate the grasses are high as a man's waist. Over the October river the plaintive 't-e-e-e' of *Chaimarrorius leucocephalus*. The Bogue forts are black with fire and smoke. For a couple of razed and looted palaces, for a nation forced to consume the cakes of a debilitating and fatal bliss, for an unequal treaty and five million ounces of silver (recriminatory indemnity) > two knighthoods. For a horde of hovering missionaries and merchants, for a yawning trade deficit > a deep and an abiding, "undermining our good customs and morality", resentment. The Bogue forts black with fire with smoke. For ten thousand released chests of seized contraband and "a barren rock". For an ignored testimonial, "Your Majesty has not before been thus officially notified … that we mean to cut this harmful drug." > In the snow's fallen silence "a hundred years of the saddest news … A road for none but the birds".

Heart of Oak

Driven from a cramped fog infested island of stewed cabbage and curses by the trade winds, by warm air of deliverance from all that tethered, restrained. Greeted by fluty song 'we-weeleow' of *Oriolus chinensis*, over bamboo thickets. Unable to transcend, though, theodolite in hand, draining swamp, drawing map, laying down road, that idée fixe: continuity within the moment's succession. Unable, that is, to see there are no permanent moments, objects. Only a catena of separate yet coordinated events, yielding one deceiving attribute after another, luring one into a permanent episode of mind, an identity fixed: upon an independent and elusive substance. Not to have discerned in that 'we-weeleow' what was a succession only of *similar* events, or notes. No song (changed interval, pitch, timber and tempo) ever sounds the same. And, further, not to have discerned that the silence in the silence which followed it was not the true silence was to have missed an opportunity unequalled. Furled in each other, silence & song, the true silence was the dissolution of *both* silence and song. Many years later, holds full of bullion, they would return. Return to a song: one which, 'ch-ee, ch-ee', identified and re-cognised always sounded the same. To an empty song in a wood with an idol placed within it. Reared with the profits from a world it divided and sacked. Bloated by half-blinding kudos. Fed on blood of wars. Gouging the earth it stood on. Its devotees a horde of hungry wasps drowning in comfitures.

Diomedea Exulans

Out of frozen wastes of sea. Precipices of water. Of years forsaking land. *Diomedea exulans*, held in the wind, sliding and pulled by the current, higher and lower. Until both the descent and the ascent seem to coincide in its 'motionless' body, which seems neither to move away from nor toward us. Whose motion, *though its beginning must be seen to occur as a thing in the present is only detectable at a point in the past or the future*, begins nowhere. 'Waa-waa-waa'. Fragment of a call, faltering in these "forever exiled waters". In dark sleet. In driving cloud. Vocable born beyond the rim of the Great World. A language we do not own or possess. Owning the oceans. Annexing the lands beneath them. Littering the seaways – where suddenly all the birds have fallen silent, the fish left. Ghosts calling from the withered land of surplus value, from a dark dream that consumes them: "Save us". Write on these planks with the ocean's pen – in that same voice that long ago he sent back across the sea to her – the names of each product. Pipes; stems fashioned from the long hollow bones of its wings. Tobacco pouches; stitched from the large webs of its feet. Slippers; sewn from its soft downy white skin.

Home

Unshrieved by song. The familiar coast welcomed them. Air full of dark chattering. Not birds but men. Wash of waves at their feet. Sound of *Turdus merula*. Flight of its note through the deep wood again. Not man but bird. Welcomed them. With a prolonged catena of sound. At its heart > they paused. They listened. The past, the present, merely a succession of events, episodes of mind. A chimera. And for a brief moment, it seemed, it was as if they had forgotten just where, "is this mine own countree?", and who, they were.

From a deep dusk. A garden. Subdued laughter. 'Plue, plue, plue.' Picus viridis. *One faded image succeeding another. Towards dawn. The ink has turned to dust. One discontinuous, scribbled note. Into the nebulous, still heart of night. Of silence.*

City of Flowering Almonds

"It is not easy to decide whether something can be in itself or whether nothing can, in which case everything is either nowhere, or in something other than itself".

Aristotle   *Physics*

From the Tin Islands we came dragging the tattered trunks of our forebears those extirpators of signs, experienced in the art of ambush, grain hoarding, supplying of boys and girls to the Palace, behind us. When first spring droughts turned the creeks' ditch hollows iron hard. From tide-washed wild-flower salterns, banks littered with cracked brinepans, where barges were hovelled wharfwards. From malarial, killpriest country. Scented sea asters edged the creeks beneath Hawkesbury. An "unstained light" filled the estuary. Came, "lusting for it like pigs". Loud talking. Our gunny sacks on our backs. Seeking the ideal city. The stale odour of a protracted adolescence spent in drawing rooms and church halls hovering about us. Ears ringing with the sound of hawsers and tramcars. Stepping out from the gloom of provincial libraries and museums. Waving goodbye to the concupiscence that festered through smoke filled afternoons of ennui frittered away in saloon bars. Leaving behind us those agues, cold sweats of the dammed heart perpetually imploring. Spring came, over the misty salterns. An eructation, an easing. From the winter's strangled heart, its frozen locks. A teasing, makeshift warmth, pretending to caress before it too departed. Leaving us slumped against each other, in a cul-de-sac, listening to the songs of those returning, from the sanctioned isles or the humid zones of the hot lands. Envy in our voices, and our vices, a deliberate swagger. Till, in the evening, exhausted by such tentative sweet shoots so reluctantly abandoned, we picked ourselves up and left. A music, written by no man's hand but in all men's minds, played to us across the fields and gardens and the allotments.

***

Praya cracked by the pipal's root. A mucked anchorage. From within the shadows of the emporium odours of many kinds of lacquered wood. Of straw and sawdust crates. Leather, rattan, ink & fermented curd. Behind glass a landscape in cork. Mucilage of vellum pads sweating. Afternoons adrift on the fragrance of earthen gods. Fortunes in calico. Cheap fabrics. Kind words – spoken to no one. Morgues filled by epidemics, plague. The profit consumes more than the loss. Hours spent in idleness on board yachts, in cheap saloons. The kuli straining at his load. Savants of the West, a dime a dozen, afloat on the tideways.

***

Out of the melancholy sucking of black water in gutters, a tessellated image: bright eyes, flecked with gold. Burning. Under the slender waist, insomnia of suburbs. Laughter bred out of boredom. The fragrance of eidos, in cold northern air, masking the stink of workhouses. Image distilled in distant & discontinuous city. Within white stones, streets and alleyways. "There is none hathe a forme so diuine / In the earth or the ayre". Or on the sea. Genuflected to before a shrine of sweating adherents.

***

In the Imperial Academy of Metals Joachim Gaunse instructs the fly on the end of his nose in the arcane assuagings of grief. In the crucible's noise everything foretold. A *sine qua non* for the Fates' opprobrium. His unheretical heart melts in the warm rose window. To solemnise the leavings of the day. A broken tooth. Appalling weather.

***

A habitation. A census: two sellers of singing finches, one geomancer, seventeen bamboo petate and grass-linen weavers, thirteen book binders, sixteen brothels, twelve apothecaries, six fortune tellers, forty opium divans, sixty rice dealers, twelve shoe makers, fifteen coconut huskers - amongst others. *Sal* > To leap. To dance; the eye's delight in it, to uncover a form of earthly perfection. Through sea mist. Through sea haze. Through too much waste and too much want.

***

On the water steps at evening fragrance of flowering almonds & apricots blown on the tide winds. Over the sandbars perfume of flowering shrubs. To a door in a high wall against which they moored they ascended from the river. Paved courtyards. Orchid Door. Connecting gateways, galleries. Groves of bamboo. Came with a desire, but no face to it. With many faces. Confused emotions. On the water steps at evening toiling avatars of no fixed abode, riding the whirlwind. Fragrance of flowering almonds & apricots. Perfume of unknown shrubs.

***

The ductile dross of a nation's adventuring, fifty two killed under ground, come round at last. Poured into its pale bloodstream. Old enmities. Joachim Gaunse, smelting for munitions. Filing, soldering, forging, casting & polishing the dream of an untarnishable city. Old strife. Figures upon a ground of "insatiate avarice". On it the wreckage of all their expeditions – grave relics, bizarre importations from strange and remote places – is piled.

***

Spring surges, again, over the misty salterns. Then slides off across the sea embankments, hot sun baking the driftways hard. Across that everlasting boundary between what proposes & what retracts. What's lent & what's (if anything) repaid. Leveraged lives. Words. Resting upon what's absent. An exhausted currency. "Tu ta ti, nu na ni" lodged in the ear of an ancient catechism. Incising accounts, recording stock. Falling and rising. "What god, man, or hero / Shall I place a tin wreath upon!" Rising. Falling. All the cedars of Lebanon.
    Marne.
                        Vistula.
            Danube.
                              Loire.
                                        Rhine.
Dammed, choked by the rafts they buoy up on their promissory currents. All the forests, gone. Up in dark smoke. "Tu ta ti, nu na ni".

***

What sweetness withheld, or withdrawn, generates the shrill sad music of carnage? Wadmerse. Salt-mire. Clegg-flies, clustered on each day's heapings of new dung, sip at the feedings. Little grows on creek head soils. Claggy terrain of red sailed hoys, run down hythes. Collier brig. Sprit-sail barge. A landscape inundated. "In dirige and masse for my soule" across backyard soakaway, swine-wood, tide-washed ear. Bundle at the wharf: 'A Man unknown'. Hooked to the sea wall. Stale pool, or puddle.

***

A flock of lacklustre gulls over rundown bayside apartments and hotels. On half lit stairs the moon proposes & discloses. Not love, but the narcotic swoon of a traveller reaching for the moon, for all the destinations on offer. *Mare Tranquillitatus*, south of the *Caucasus Mountains*, on an Aryanised terrain. No. Not quite. But, in the hush that follows, the tropical night delivers, in a sudden backwash of kisses, this refrain: 'then there suddenly appeared before me, the only one my arms will ever hold. I heard someone whisper please adore me, and when I looked the moon had turned to gold'.

***

"I do not find nor have I ever found any writings of the Romans or Greeks which give definitely the position in the world of the earthly paradise". Signs. Signs inscribed in the margins of a phantasmal geography. Wish-horizon. Celestial drawer of maps.

***

For that "great cacique of the north", black eyes holding him in thrall, burning, in the white of a virgin's complexion, he would contend at furious headwaters in small boats: with "billow and terrible current", drought and scarcity, loss of sea anchors, death. Would, finding such "aboundance as in the first creation", with "bars, sledges [and] wedges of iron" prise open, slowly, the ground of her great veins and ores, delving and easing his hands in her fine sludges & grains, sluicing her streams' gravels, rich alluviums, sands & rocks. Until, awash in her great waters again, settled on her soft banks and shores, he delivered "a way ... to answer every mans longing".

***

An unmapped island found us tossing all night at sea by day floundering in our bunks. Navigating a way beyond the farthest reaches of our compass. Flatus Vocis we called it. Bare scarp. Waterless rock. A place clinging to no name – the presence of a name not necessarily bestowing, upon what its mere sound proposes, a reality. We planted our keel in the surf of a bank of deep and brightly lisping shingle. Later we would follow our noses through a swamp of crab apples and lice, scattering the seeds of our syllables, swinging a cutlass our nervous host waiting suppliant at the door as if he had known all along that we were journeying to meet him. That night we lay awake on deck under the stars. The air was full of noises: singing from flower-boats, banter from ear cleaners; more sombre intoned voices from floating pharmacopoeias, hewers and suppliers of coffins. Like a bright sheet of dented white tin the sea during the day. The lisping white water over the shingle. We smoked, we cursed, we climbed into the rigging. A nameless thirst, out of the acrid stink of the salt-thick sea, ate into our being. Taking possession of ourselves, at last, our destinies before us, we landed. A fly on an epaulet angrily and haughtily harangued us.

Ethnological Curiosities

"Thou shalt not sow thy field with mingled seed."

Leviticus 19:19

One

Alone in this dead city by the salt marsh. City I long to leave. City I long to return to. Each morning workers coughing on their way to the factory. Each evening mist over the quiet quays. After the export trade declined. Importers now of oil and wood, of electronics and food. After the sea withdrew its bounty from us. Exporters of spent uranium and industrial waste. Poisonous rains at twilight. The river with its dead dogs. Two blocks away the Mint, the Ministry of Financial Services. Close by, the Archive of Ethnological Curiosities. And beside it, the Numismatic Museum: behind dressed granite generation after generation of the country's Kings and Queens, Emperors and Empresses, pseudo Sultans and Satraps, their heads embossed in gold. From far flung corners of the globe. A collective effulgence. Now, in the gloom of yet another polluted evening they shine, if at all, with a less than vigorous light. I stand on the balcony, smoking. All traces of the day's deliria having subsided from the roads beneath me. Like a painted mime faces linger in doorways and in shop windows, each one having pursued his or her "separate interest and pleasure". Each one reluctant to go home. The faces of a city that has died, that has been reborn and has died again. In its canals the waters, still, forgetful and habitual. Dark as the ink of any actuary or obituary. The great warehouses gone. Docks and schools turned into luxury apartments – still vacant. The wind rattles through deserted goods yards at dawn. The bodies of dead soldiers returning. Rumours of another war. Of borders sealed and people fleeing. No love amongst the populace of a common good at home. Even less of it for those abroad; exploited, murdered or pauperised by those we elected. In cemeteries of de-consecrated churches, in parks, on wayside verges, autumn encamps. Blood red coppices emblazon air. Days shorten. Mist wraps viaducts and bridges. I lean on the balcony, dreaming. Sound of an oratorio through an apartment's broken window. A solitary drunk walks down the side of the road, unseeing. No one pays him any attention. In the canals the waters have begun to harden. Harden around this present. Present which perpetually returns. With a yesterday and a tomorrow; in an unbroken circuit. Taking its place amidst all time's other inventions and appearances. Here, on these roads which no longer vibrate to the triumphal return of armies, it waits, like a foul shadow between the houses, trying to extinguish itself. Enveloping us, too, in its disguises. Seeking, like the stale Ithaka in our bones, a home. Which we, through the grace of our fictions of memory and experience, always provide for it. An exhausted destination. Standing at the door, beckoning us to follow. And we comply. Turning back again to the contaminated moment; of an evening plundered by love, indifference or hate. The grey gestation of the day to come, much like the one before. So it was, though they did not know it, when long ago they set out, from other wharves than the ones here now. Dead men singing on the current. Cadavers, not angels, for burying. Men whose narratives would never be completed. Completion requiring surrender. Surrender to what was beyond them. Not suffering – for surfeit of profit or passion. As they left they heard a song above the osier-beds. Fiercely compressed as if it desired never to be repeated. 'Acrocephalus palustris', marsh warbler, singing in a voice reconstituted from all its migrations; each syllable, each phrase, a locus. Singing a song reinscribing in itself the songs of many others. Stumbling through ruined villages at dusk, half full of vermin, they imagined they still heard it. Through fields of unharvested wheat. Presiding at baptisms in remote mountain gorges. Whilst climbing paths treading wild garlic and jasmine into the dust, the sea behind them, before them a fragile carapace of snow and ice – cerement of crystal. No looking back. Whilst scrambling over dry river courses, then down amid arid plains welcomed by horse traders and hunters – for a lame piebald with a downcast look which moved them they bartered a silver fork – through landscapes without cities, without boundaries. Into those immensities of unnavigated, and unrecorded, space and light.

***

"[June 21st 1645] A long strand broke upon us, suddenly, out of the sea mist and it was as if in that perfect parabola of sand and foam, that gently sluiced light – O sempiternal referent! – the accumulated rime of all those years sea-wandering was lifted from our eyes. Here, we thought, amidst sweet solaceful scents wafted offshore from some ripe and verdant interior, is the beginning of that world of limitless possibility we had imagined. Day after day, year after year, watching the horizon for sign of some such land, our very selves poured on ahead into the distance, our minds nurtured on the prospect of the destruction of all boundaries. The Absolute, in a form, we veritably believed, of some demiurge or afflatus, beckoned. Only our ever sanguine and sceptical Doctor, Peter Vanderhoeven, cautioned that we might well be pursuing nothing more than residual effects of repeated calenture, or of insufflation of the nerves brought on by too much confinement. 'That unconstrained condition which you seek, too, is not natural. And …' he added as an aside, I suspect, upon all our 'continual exploring … the whole person is never completely anywhere.'"

.....

"[December 12th 1645] On the night air were the odours of grilled meats and the sounds of far off dancing and music. In life, according to the good Doctor, whose discourse inherits the complexion of the Philosopher, one is either moving away from something or someone, there is either a leave taking, or one is moving towards them in impending arrival. Attraction or repulsion, terror or joy, we move, within ourselves, always between opposed or different states and emotions – our being never exclusively engaged within either. Arriving, we are also departing, departing, we are also arriving, and in this slow sad music in which all our lives are conducted there are only impure journeys, imperfect divagations, towards a union which always eludes us. So the horse traders settled down with us outside the walls of the city of the ancient kingdom, their mallets pounding tent pegs into hard earth, as dark lanterns swayed in the breeze and braziers of spluttering coals glowed red in the dusk."

[From *Journals of the Expeditions of Sir John Faversham*]

***

Beneath me, on the street, a faint burnishing light. Late November. Cold gleam upon the window. Gulls, blown from the headland by the sea wind. Chalk-white underparts burning, luminous against deep bruise-blue sky. I listen to their cries above dull accents from the street below. Axles grind the air. A gust of wind, thick with the smell of saw-mills and crude oil from refineries, fills the balcony. Under the passing darkness of a squall newspapers and litter are lifted and threshed down emptying streets. Close by a dog howls from a vacant lot. A broken latch bangs on the security gate of a boarded-up beauty parlour. Above the increasing tumult I imagine I catch, for one brief moment, a shard of frenetic song; Acrocephalus palustris, wringing its repertoire of motifs above the osier-beds. Beds where pill-boxes still stand, crumbling on jetties. Where once, damp days among the fens, they waited: time, monotonous and cruel. A continent on fire, a people burning. "Minds bent on a debauchery of destruction ... a boisterous joy." Windows blacked out. Beyond the saltings dark breakers overwhelmed.

Two

Container/trailer-loads of trinkets & gadgets for an insatiable populace. Inflamed appetency. Blight of consumption. At intervals along the estuary container ports (there is no shrine without a pilgrimage undertaken) where once there were ferry crossings and fordings for sacred destinations. Through scurvy-grass/sea aster/osier-bed up through dense forests, paths beaten by pilgrims. Bare feet on the rutted highway - its slipper chapels, shrines, hospitals and pyxides of martyr's water - bruised, lacerated, chastened.

***

I stand alone on the balcony looking out over the city. At mud banks flickering, flashing on the river. At vandalised telephone booths and bus shelters. At the many disguises time assumes. Listening, in the noise of each moment, arising and departing before me, for the sound of things long dead, and to come. From another November, perhaps, as distant and obscure as the pier-heads and bus stations buried under shrouds of mist. Above the balcony an eider duck ascends, heading north. The osier-beds are silent, empty. The city is filled with the sounds of departure. Only in the low, rancorous calls of its pedestrians does it recognise the sound of that recurring present of which it is composed. That moment of repetition and recuperation, in which it asserts itself. In which all of its endless grey days and suffocating nights are exhaled upon the minds of those it inhabits. Whose destiny it shapes and unfolds. City, set astride the illusion that time is infinitely malleable and renewable. Upon its bridges, in its arcades, the visitor lingers and thinks they hear, in its wide avenues and in its squares set back from them, a music of perfect intervals, cadence of stone and air, the absolute architecture of their dreams.

***

By their own beliefs those who set out from salt-eaten quays were corrupted. Fuellers of time and all its fevered and importunate forms. Engravers of 'pathless winds'. Within the mangrove. Upon the beach with the waterfall. Too much diversity, as if each thing began and ended with itself, demanding too much understanding from them. Lost without water on endless northern plains, stumbled upon by itinerant gatherers of horse droppings. Terror subsiding beneath too much joy. Too much joy subsiding beneath what could not contain it.

***

Over the rooftops, dull gleam of the estuary. On the opposite bank on a horizon of low hills, tall stacks darkly etched, the oil refineries stand in a swathe of late evening light. Drifting down the long gilded stream of air in a billowing procession, a massed riot of cloud; an orange, purple, slate-grey conflagration. It seems to move as if in accord with some deep and urgent compulsion. Because it does so at a height, seemingly, barely above that of the refineries, it appears as if the conflagration issues, there being no smoke without fire, from their stacks. As if all the planet's ancient petrified forests were transpiring again upon the air their brief lives. Burning, in that dark oleaginous element to which they had been consigned, with a bright apocalyptic fury; spreading an ominous red glow over the hills beyond the city.

Envoi

Love, that fragment which attracts, sought after in every gaze and sign, that incompleteness which always goes in search of an other, within whose field of gravitation it is ineluctably pulled. Moving in fear of assassination each night from one official residence to another, only a handful of trusted aides knowing where he slept. Paid informants in every household. The highways, resplendent in summer, lined with elm and locust trees. All set to a common gauge, width of rut. Along them, through the high plains, the passes, deserts and islands, through the far prefectures and vassalages, it called; dust darkening its habiliments. Nothing begins, or ends, in itself.

Between the River and the Sea

"What do I perceive? Forms. And what besides? Forms. Of the substance I know nothing. We walk among shadows, ourselves shadows to ourselves and to others".

Diderot *Elements of Physiology*

One

Charged to take possession of all "the lands, woods, soile, groundes, havens, ports, rivers, mines, mineralls, marshes, waters, fishinges, commodities and hereditamentes whatsoever" found by them. H.M.S. *Terra Incognita* slips her hawser at the Great Dock. Wharves of the capital dissolve in grey light behind her. Pennant of Company aflutter on the breeze. Sails out into the estuary mouth. Bright creel of water > syllable of sea, or river? Not both, in the same place at the same time. The one, sea-water, arriving, then, after the other has gone. If so what's left: a river abandoned by fresh water, by that without which it cannot exist. Sea-water occupying what is name-less. Sails, therefore, into a further incognito. Unexcavated space. Pennant hanging limp at the rail. No breeze stirring. The current still.

***

O heavenly Pilot guide us, and our frail craft, to that uninscribed space so that we may with rostrum and stylus write on it, as on a blank page, the names of a geography.

**

Two

Hawsers hold the frayed cordage of a dream > *syllable* > *word* > sentence. Fragment of a sound, held in the ear. Carrying it with them. Syllable of augury, omen. Sing, syllable > of those white granite quays you set out from, with a shifting cargo of salt and ground husks, caulked with oakum, with a tattered sail riding the crests of each seething hill of water. Of those white endless spaces breath took root in, phonic substratum of all words, amid frozen steppe and drifting sand-bar, under immense sky. Sing > of how such momentary partite sounds could produce a cargo of such mentation, such permanent value.

***

On the way from El-Kanais, on the Edfu-Berenice road, a graffito was left at the Pan temple asking for a safe journey … Sing, *beyond* the activity of speech *beyond* what is named and name-less, how beside the date groves, bearing gifts of spikenard, costus and bdellium, down the green and fertile valleys of the ear – the wrath bearing spirit of the incense tree could not be appeased – you lost your way amidst so much diversity. And how, after charred orchard, dried-up ox bow lake and braided channel, plied with libations of kumiss, delicate powdered bones of gazelle, you were ship-wrecked, and were traded.

***

Names dim on headstones, atop a bluff in a small churchyard overlooking a creek of the estuary. Late November light. A bird sings on a threadbare branch. Windblown note tossed over mudbanks. Then another. Weaving a coppice of sound, where no coppice is, in leafless air; a pattern. Name in damp sandstone weathers to mist again. Breath-crossing. From shore to shore borne ceaselessly forwards and backwards, seeking itself.

***

Sold and bought, traded and transplanted. A system of classification: class, order, genus, species. A hierarchy of want (standardize, at any cost) and discrimination. "A great botanical exchange house for the empire". Botany giving the lie to booty - now a traded commodity > pace beauty. An eclipse of voices. From *Talisay* (leaves oviate, tapering, ripening to yellow) > *Almendras* > *Dalinsi* > > *Baadaam* > *Deshi badam* > *Jangli badam* >> *Ketapang* >> *Kaathe badaam* >> via *Umbrella Tree* > *Malabar almond* > *Seabean tree* > to, simply, *Terminalia catappa*. Terminal of want. A name sold and bought.

***

Sing, syllable. Of how in those high mountain passes thralled by air of transhumance, you descended. Your sound a scatter of pebbles amid loose screes; ripple, glitter of water through steep villages, deities paraded up tracks to flute and drum. Descended; amid salt trader, caravan leader and mint-master. Amid accountant, stocktaker, night-watchman, scribe. To fumigations, embalmings and haruspications. To an ornate erotica and a muddy road.

***

Three

In half-light a bird sings. Out over tide-washed saltern, neither land nor water, its note hangs. Wind pulled fragment. Invisible flotsam. From the edge of dark and light, of pain and joy, weaving above mud banks. Forlorn, and exultant. In half-light. Limpid desideratum.

***

Bow-heave. Squall blacked mizzen. Out of the south, south east, or east south east. On deck names tilt, slide, are re-calibrated. To agree with tide, wind, current. Course and time of arrival. Wave-word, not sensation, breaks over mind and body: attributes deferred, substance promoted. But where 'river' ends and 'sea' begins no cognisor can determine.

***

Tide-wash over misted quay. Ghostly rigging. *Syllable:* knotted, and mooring. Cast off into marsh breath. *Word*: hawse-block to keep sea out, maintain order. When they set off the willows were drooping with spring. They returned, annealed in dark waters of dichotomies. *Sentence*: 'extermination' > "simply another name for natural selection". Winter grinding their words. Afraid of nothing: of what is nameless, incognito.

***

Between the river and the sea a pennant hangs limp at a rail. No breeze stirs. The current is still. A bird sings from a far shore. An absence is only within a mute presence revealed. In wordless air, then, what syllable's dissolved, what song restored?

The Bee Wood

"I shall give thee ... the uttermost parts of the earth
for thy possession".
Psalms 2:8

One

In the bee wood <*medhu> a sweet music <melitos> is produced.

***

The verges of dirt track and back road are littered with empty six-packs. Shadows move before us. Roiling like prairie fire across borders. Through half-light our Winnebagos pitch and roll. In the house of dust we are dreaming, dreaming still of a sweet music, a honeyed tongue. A music white <*bha-l-tos> as snow, and shining.

***

Turn the radio up. Listen to the news of another new war, insurgency or uprising. Beirut is burning. The ancient fragments of columns blown into the air land again upon your sill. A bright morning. Incandescent. But no one is listening.

***

This wheel turns all the way from the wagon grave at Lukynova where it was buried – sing us your five-thousand-year-old songs imitating the calls of birds, your pastoralist's dream creaking above dowelled planks – to the highway beside Grand Rapids Falls. At *itchyfeet.biz* click on > Mobile Homes. Then click on > Honey Wagon.

***

Tap your feet on the floor. All the dancers are waltzing westward. Everything flows – in the same direction > from that first great murderous Macedonian surge, *sal* lying forth. We are *Selyenes*, a dancing, tripping, marching people. And we have all been mouthing - with our post 1786 philologists – the language of paradise.

***

Listen. At the end of the road, where once they were herded like cattle and the smoke from their lodges darkened the sky, they are singing. In *The Iron Horse* Psychic Suzanna is telling the fortunes of overweight Caucasians. They are dining on chips. To a music of roulette wheels and gaming machines operated by a people who foraged once for kelp and mussels along shore and tidal creek.

Two

Nothing resides and inheres within itself, but is the sum of its attributes.

***

Each evening through the long nights of summer we listen, for a lost music. Above neatly trimmed hedgerows, above the dull light that flickers at the end of the patio, it is rising. Like the shine of melt water when the world thawed. Above lawns and inessential houses, across borders haunted by the scent of honeysuckle, it moves.

***

Over the white fields the colours of the world roll. Explosions daily rattle its windows. The breath of perfidious dichotomies occludes them. Out of the ditch its *Systema Naturae*: white/yellow/red/black (in that order) climbs, its *anima mundi*, and will not go back.

***

Sound of panel beaters, engines, car horns, newspaper sellers > vagabond music. Hand raised eye afloat on one moment moving into the next. Each note a departure from and a returning to what it is not. Inaudible scale through which the world turns; in which to deny is to affirm, somewhere else, what can't be seen or heard. Until each sound and object begins only where it ends. Sucking the bones of such music. Dissolved in it.

***

Someone is singing, beyond the patio and the hedgerow, a song so sweet it might have been sung in paradise. Inconsolable *melos*. A lyric in a strange tongue. It sounds like part elegy, part yearning. Like someone nostalgic, perhaps, for a lost continent, beginning.

Three

Snow falls on empty silos. In the derelict rooms of houses. In the spaces between boarded up towns. A ghost train whistles. Over the vanished hunting grounds of the departed.

***

Who journeyed there before us out of the house of dust? Refugees from dust. Northward. Their tracks erased. Eyes raised > to the gull's wing tipped with white from the empyrean. For words. Words. On handbills and on posters. Promising. Promising.

***

Dream sign. Border or boundary. A crossing > from one exile into a next. A home-coming. Deliver us from horseflies, anxieties of dusks and woods. Provide us, instead, with some limitless expanse.

***

Not to return   those same longings.

tu ta ti   nu na ni

to those same monsters

***

In those White Snow Lands <*bha-l-tos> on the blank pages of the ear, nothing is > independent of attributes, nothing is > beyond fear beyond hope > in the white tracts of non-contra diction > diction itself dispersed.

Wind sows, breath reaps, beyond all mutable categories and grammars. Blows, what's lost what's found again and lost, in equal measure. What wheels and turns in the immense silence and distance. In those empty Snow Lands, whose shadows move before us. Turning back continuously, stopping and looking at us. Turning and looking and saying: "Why are you waiting?"

Obsequy for Lost Things

(2014)

"It is only delusion, and not knowledge, that bestows happiness."
Stefan Zweig

The Lower Reaches

"This is England, and I'm in a nice, clean English room with all the dirt swept under the bed".

Jean Rhys

One

I

After the high pitched whine of bellicosity: "We'll bomb you back to the stone age" the remote is pressed. Crackle of distressed air. Warm, incendiary smell. All colour implodes to a white mote. Silence. The crevasse opens.

II

Boiling white spume. Caught on steps of the public baths before noon, the shadow of a vapour. Ash, in the dissolved hand. Shard, or ember. All melted into air. In the stone, heart's cold memento.

III

What keel breaks this ice? What *dignitas* is affirmed in these particulars of a profound winter? Our Lady of the Salterns bless this rotting wharf, this ramshackle back-end deserted by the tides. It is snowing over all the reed clogged wet-lands of the earth.

IV

Scent of sea asters edged the creek. "Die tankanlagen" under the aimer's sight. "Marschland." Identified/located from a great height. Locked in a grid: "Zu den Sachen Selbst!" Held for a moment in his gaze, they bled. Blackened viscera. The air received them.

V

Outside the window purple reeded hollows of the former fleet. Sea lavender, grey with river light. At the inlet's mouth, where a "leakinge, unwholesome ship" once harvested wind, tide lapped silt bars catching the sun's last rays ignite. As, too, the scarp's high ledge of flowering thorn – a "Sea-mark", Hawkesbury-bush > Hamechesburga > burh: *hill*. The Hill of the Hawks.

VI

Togodumnus. Dead or lost amidst the reed beds. Harried from fen to fen. His horses slain. Pursued into the claggy wastes east of the Island of Thorns. Aiming beyond the sand capped wooded heights perhaps for Camulodunum, he disappeared. Sound of the bittern booming amid bull rushes. Slither of sword hilt and shield, as each man sought to hold his footing through the miry labyrinth. Water welded to sky. On the driving salt wind the sound of men closing. Panick, then stumbling. A foreign tongue. There is gold in Dalcouthi.

VII

Over the mudflats the smell of oil. Dream of an ideal order. Beyond any particular geography, any particular time or place at all. Driving men mad. Blacking the shore. Leveraging the sea-lanes open. "A perpetuall warre without peace or truce." Crude. Pungent in summer, over the fields and hedgerows. And in the houses of the villages. Ancient distillate. Of a mind which "(save upward to the heavens) could have little solace or content in respecte of any outward objects."

Two

I

Out of the forlorn city at last, its fogs and its counting houses. The white noise in the rigging after dark. Droning. Insincere. Incessant. Past Thorn Island where one summer the effluvium became too much even for those inside debating. Each voice overlapping and merging with the other. And with those outside, reporting. Downstream. Past Hole Haven. Scent of sea lavender on the breeze. White noise in the rigging. Smell of the open sea roads. Stars look down on another journey about to be undertaken.

II

Struggling through deep drifts with a copy of *Der Angriff* under his arm, a latter day Robert Conway. Ice fragments from the Pontic steppes lodged deep in the tread of his boots, his shadow survives in abattoirs and in the stockyards of railway terminuses. In the frozen breath of *die Kristallnacht*. But who has not followed and extolled, through a bloodied swathe of foreign villages and towns, that small red rowan on his cheek, "that nobly arched head, containing such a quantity of brain … those coral lips?"

III

Driftway, sluice. Beyond, breakwater, river scour, margin. Where foreland of saltern is over-lapped. "All overflowen". And eyot, and terp: "quite drowned". No tithe map of any use. No tiltboat to stairs or wharf. Undrained. Unforded. What soggy track, inter-coursed with copse/willow, to follow? All wetland words, and ways, converge; seem foreign. To find a way, amid shifting brine sump, piling, hollow.

IV

Togodumnus. Feet in mud. Following the channel's curve. Seeking the higher ground. Above the sedge lapped verge his shadow flits. Gulls cry out over the sunken tideway. Revenge. But there are no tracks to guide him back. Each imprint erased in the flood's quiet launder.

V

For "a pug nosed rodent with lustrous fur", for a pile of moth eaten pelts, the "beaver fields exhausted", the great Eastern deciduous forest depleted, a civilisation, with no concept of wealth accumulation, "debauched".

VI

Shiver and sweat of tidewrack. Limbs blue. Cold flicker on silt bank. Slippage of foot. Through Flat and Ooze. Where the river "enters the Ocean" – "carelessly camped upon its bank". *In avia secutus.* Head spun. Heart colder. To bend, finally, at Claudius' foot. Not dead. A survivor. REG MAG IN BRIT. An instrument, *reges et amici*, of the imperium. Benefactor, and supporter, of an ideal order.

VII

Sun dappled worm-eaten wharf in a wilderness of water and sky. Where the "aguish miasma" rose after sun dip. Where the starch collared pilot set out under the sand capped scarp. Light on hedgebank, on fill dyke. To guide far off destinies afloat through treacherous shoals, sands. For a country intent, at any cost, on extending its reach. *Oppidum.* Power point. Wooden pile driven into the mud.

VIII

'Big swinging dicks' amid the rigging. All hands below aloft chipping ice off a top heavy vessel. The ice-master frantic. All Libor rates 'fixed'. "A ... culture rotten with cynicism and greed." From the Hill of the Hawks, what eye looks down?

IX

A journey endlessly postponed. In the leather lined clubs of its capital. At regattas, tattoos and royal enclosure. In "cultivate[d] nostalgia". In the Honours list nailed to the door. In expurgated diaries of heroes who "swear all day at [their] companions" and are transformed into "splendid failure[s]". In 'lost' government archives. In the inherited and laundered loot of families and State. In a mythos of fairness assiduously cultivated and disposed. By an emasculated corps of vendors of 'news'. By a plethora of anointed insouciants.

X

From le Hole havene, "in very deep and current free water at maximum practicable distance from the coast ... the files ... in weighted crates", *And specially from every shires ende / Of Engelond ... they wende* past gut and hedgebank, creekside and shore, on "perambulation", prayers offered en route, pollard "bounds trees" freshly scored or mutilated, on occasion youths ceremoniously scourged so they would remember a significant location, "by the time I cut his balls off ... he had no ears and his eyeball, the right one, I think, was hanging out of its socket", mapping the "Bounds of the parish". Three and a half tons of what "might embarrass" the government, and "whose existence ... should never be revealed." Scent of sea lavender over the mud. "... he died before we got much out of him". Smell of the open sea roads.

XI

Our Lady of the Salterns bless this rotting wharf, this ramshackle back-end deserted by the tides.

In the Year of Expeditions

"We are filled with homesickness for no identifiable home."
James Hamilton-Paterson

Interlocutors of silences. On a still night. What eye's afloat. What heart's adrift. Upon a fragment. A phantom.

***

From swampy, tide-washed wild flower salterns where the creek once bent by Lady's Island, poling with long oars up torturous narrows.

***

In our minds that "implacable blancheur"; unmapped, untrodden. Flower of a cold lattice, on which the wave breaks.

***

Across the horizon History marches. Shadows weep. From the Archive of Paradise a rare bird. In its beak – exquisite plumage! – bright petals. In the ashes of their extinguished fires we warmed our feet. All night the surf a faded enfilade across the reef.

***

Expedition of vanishings. Air beaten to airy thinness. From the alembic of the Word flesh and bone excised. Each thing that we extolled we removed. A fragrance hung on the world.

***

At night in our dreams a strange figure came toward us. Then stopped. From the alder swamp by the dim light of the creek head it waved. It pronounced upon us all the blessings of whiteness.

***

And Joas Croppenburgh, and Giles Vanderputt, held back the sea for us. Day after day we heard, amidst sallow willow in the deep field ditch, it rage.

***

Over their ruined roads only phantoms returned. A catatonia of shadows. Their memories torn out.

***

Suddenly one night in our dreams she turned up. Unannounced. Forgotten. To claim, she said, all the gods, and all the songs, we had taken from her.

***

A new land, smelling sweeter than all the rest. The small boat we put over the side, to claim it. The exclamations of astonishment. What the wave brought back. The chimera's gaze. Bilge of eviscerated doubt.

***

A hoarse aubade. In the contused throat. Note flung out over settlements of stones and charred femurs. A settled gloom. What ear, before dark, will hear that voice, before it is gone forever?

***

Over all the horizons of the dead the wind has fallen silent. It is snowing. The arquebuses have dissolved. All the codices have been wiped clean. No one leaves any footprints. No one arrives or departs.

***

Through damp backlands, where ditch side reed was in season, by old Dutch embankments, by steadings where hazel and dogwood loomed lush and full, by Marsh bailiff Zacharia Button's cottage, in the Year of Expeditions.

***

No journey's end. No end to looking. But under the moon we raised up a giant gallows. Harvested pain. We sharpened our blades upon them.

***

All the names erased – from plinth and citadel. Salt eaten. Vestige of a world, returned to silence. They were 'Sojourners in the land' only. Inheriting the Ocean.

***

Could you not hear, could you not smell those shadows jostling with their rotting cadence through the skin of their depredations. Inscribed on the bones of the living, and the dead. Draped in a deep distemper. Entering the graveyard?

***

Murmurings, expostulations in the dark. But the orders have been promulgated. The street names changed. No evidence, no signs of a crime committed. All outward destinations are the same.

***

Stir to the sheer cry of a gull driven by the sea's raging. Haunting cry. Wreathed in high wrought balconies between sleep and waking. A cry reminding us of home.

***

When will wheat ripen on rises above the saltern's edges. Its shadow wave in the breeze. Beyond, above high perched Hawkesbury, in the rain that will fall without stopping. Where stalk and root will rot, if left, in the ground?

***

In the snow only the wind knows the names of those who are always weightless, who are always disappearing.

Obsequy for Lost Things

"The weather of these northern districts is so changeable that, even with my experience, it is impossible to foretell the sky of tomorrow."
Matsuo Bashō

A bird sings. Above a frozen river. It is neither evening, nor morning. Ancient, valedictory syllables whisper on the wind.

***

All the borders are closed. Or dissolved. No more promiscuously trafficking across them. All the signposts are buried, or are pointing the wrong way.

***

Sounds of a tongue on crisp, ice fringed margins. The rustle of a page is not as loud as the silence of the departed.

***

Here no voice emits a call for the mounting of an expedition. The dead hussar is enshrined in the glass of the glacier. He is pointing his horse toward a dark cloud on the horizon.

*

Silence drifts. Across the frozen river a sound of a bird. In the geography of all absent things things that are about to appear are forgotten.

***

It is neither morning, nor evening. It is neither winter, nor summer, autumn nor spring.

***

Only later did we realise we had been walking backwards and forwards across the border without knowing it was there.

***

Everyone is walking, in worn out boots, back to a country they do not remember but which they have been exiled from.

***

A 'People without Space'. Rose through the lean decades of hunger and of fear. Their wheel ruts visible for miles. Smoke from their campfires lingering for days, years.

***

Among the shadows. Deer barked. Fear. A mistle-thrush sang. Wind ruffled a field of grain there was no one to cut.

***

Voices, through an echo chamber of unresolved identities. Through space and time. Echoes of a place forgotten. Or, blood-mired, eschewed. "I pluck the bitter herb by the ruined wall." Exiled amidst the fragments. The contingent, 'unreal' deposits of time.

***

Leaves rustle on tumuli. A barbecue of bodies. Here everything was remembered. And everything was forgotten. In the "fathomless gulf of avarice" the border was drawn and re-drawn each minute, each hour.

***

Country of the lost. A sweating incubus slowly devouring night. The voices of those who 'disappear' grow hoarse in the throats of the living. They have swallowed a blankness too large for them to bear.

***

The land unploughed, unfenced. Hence 'unpeopled', 'vacant'. No footprint discerned. On the leafy sunlit ridge above the river. Sour Wood. Sumac. Buck-eye. Freedom of the unconstrained. Forsaking frontiers and borders for where there are none ... Dark neurotica of a dream.

***

Snow falls. Indiscriminately across borders. Covering road, fence, field. White crystal cantor. In whose freezing breath the unbuttressed takes flight. Obsequy for lost things.

***

Inside, prints of ferns on frosted panes. Door left half open. Broken chairs and trestle. Outside, empty chicken coup. Kindling wood left in the lane. A silence not heard before.

***

Flurbereinigung. Footprints of a foul chimera in mud. All the leaves had turned red. A bird sang deep in woods. It was snowing again – over roads and walls and fields. Over all the empty spaces.

***

A journey to nowhere. Over worn out roads. On dusty verges, in roadside ditches, small hands wove the rain into a repository of silence.

***

Exiled amidst fragments, contingent 'unreal' deposits of time, the light is forever changing. Endlessly, amidst tumuli of broken stones and columns, coming. And, endlessly, going.

***

A bird sings. Above a frozen river. It is neither morning, nor evening. It is snowing. It is neither summer nor winter, autumn nor spring.

Ice Stylus

(2017)

"How art thou come to this dark coast?"
Ezra Pound   *The Cantos*

Crooked Gulch

"I did not know then how much was ended."
Heȟáka Sápa (*Black Elk*)

The river's banks littered with ruined sacrariums, naves. The great walls gone: "very cumbrous to deface." Bodies taut under beams. Charred rafter. Blackened stone. Confiscated lands. Whole towns pulled down. Commons enclosed. *Unerwünscht.* Vagabonds. Only to become (some indentured) voyagers. Expropriators, inscribers of 'blank' spaces. On salt laden wind listening for the cries of land birds. Of surf pounding.

***

Names dissolved in the wind. "Roote[d] out from being." Inaudible breathings.

***

A land "free from blot or mixture." The whole of Europe dreaming. The same dream.

***

Peach and apple orchards, fields of corn. Burned, without pity. Storehouses full of squash, dried corn and beans. Houses with old men, women and children in them. "The stinck and sente … frying in the fryer." The ability to subsist depleted. Surviving on bark and roots. Hunger a hard knot of iron. "Let them eat grass."

***

A fluke of rusted iron in the heart. Poisons the tongue. Infects the hand that writes.

***

Scorn – on the white word. Shrivelled and parched. Wintering in the throat. From "the land where no one weeps." Land of eternal immiseration of snows.

***

Word: umbilicus. Nourished in earth. Our village. Our valley. Seed shadow. The sound of its root-edness. Pleasing to us.

***

Those who fell, in a black ash swamp beside a river, far from home. They had a pallor like freshly fallen snow on their hands and feet.

***

Entire villages erased from the map. At evening, in the quietness of dusk, the Names.

***

"Black-earth country." The land sings. You could smell it on their breath. And when we left there were no more trails to follow.

***

Wading, knee deep at times, through snow. For months. Our bodies frozen. The sick and old stumbling after. The young in our arms and on our backs. In the dead of winter. Desiring food and shelter. Receiving only hard looks.

***

"Seized … driven off like wolves", the sacred fires in our lodges extinguished, "turning for one last look as [we] crossed the ridge". Later the skin on our feet would break. Flies lay eggs in our lacerations. On our breath our names would become barely recognizable.

***

The land. The land sings. But not, any longer, our songs. Our streams have all fallen silent.

***

Our most private parts, man woman and child, on the crowd thronged road back into the cheering town, excised, draped over hat and pommel.

***

Ssippi. Our syllable water. Each letter a seed. Flowing through us. The land. Giving way to it. Touching, the tongue. Sound-shadow. Breath. Of a name. Askunessippi. All trace of it expunged from the map. To "cut off Remembrance of [us] from the Earth." Syllable. River. Syllable-shadow. "Hear me … For I may never call again."

***

"Spring … every seed awakened … we yield to our neighbours, even our animal neighbours, the same right … to inhabit this land." Ground. Of all being. Of what *is*.

***

Tonight the ice clad spruce taps at the window as we move beneath it silent as ghosts. "The snow drift[ing] deep in the crooked gulch" remembers.

Ice Stylus

"Everything is real, and not real,
Both real and not real,
Neither real nor not real."
Nagarjuna

I

Here there are no true travellers, only wanderers through the lands, and the towns, of middle dimensions. Stemmers of the flow, launchers of those deluded "venture[s] against the unknown". Tamers of the non-existent "wilderness".

***

Maps. The Thule – *Ultima* – of an imagination threatened. Engineers. Surveyors. Spies. Of a hideous vacuum. *Vacui*. Deep in the heart. "Love of possession was a disease with them."

***

"Qallunaat" over the freezing floe. $11000 for a dry biscuit. Thinking they were navigating amidst things rather than representations of them. What *manitou* under the auctioneer's gavel lingers?

***

Silk handkerchiefs, hair comb, scented soap, slippers, books. All that was left beneath the missing oarlocks. And a desperate note in a cairn. Somewhere far back in the frozen distance. A kettle of English flesh. The bones sang: "Don't give us anymore that rot about superior values."

***

Ice stylus. Sea Stylus. We carry the turning world in our hand. Write on it, as we please. Spelling its names backwards. Listening to them. Forged escriture of a god. As if they were owned by us.

***

Celebrity anchors. Big shot correspondents. Gucci medallions. Armani suits. Mapping a way amidst apparitions, fleeting phantoms of conjoined moments. Assembling theodolites, malls. In their hands the 'great vanities, dreams and shadows of this vanishing life.'

***

We woke in the porticos of an unexplored, largely unknown land. In our pockets nothing but the faded paper currency of our dreams. And when we looked back we saw that the way we came was simply the retracing of a worn out route.

***

"Fie. Fie." said the rollers breaking over our bows. "Do you not remember the frigate-bird on sun swept atolls its eyes burned out looking into the white plume, the blossoming white-hot cloud of darkness, of nothing? ... Do not forget the frigate-bird."

***

Will what we seize, eventually, mock and forsake us? Each border we inscribe round ourselves crumble? On the staircase when we return will there be no one at the top to greet us? Only, descending, the taciturn remnant of a life that is walking from order into disorder without us?

***

To drive "away black care", regular streets and macadamed roads. Order. Mind (city of god city of planning) divinely aloof from what it proposes.

***

"Themed weekends". From the car park tumulus of a dead king. To the Blue Badge guide. To the aerial gondola. Aloft. Aloft. Set sail. Itineraries for scented isles. Strange incantations. Auguries of refulgence. Heading east into the self-same seas where cartographers, once, drew islands that didn't exist. Which explorers repeatedly reported sighting.

***

Adrift upon summer's indolent waters. Warm waters of an atoll. Upon an air of distressed contours. Will our boat crunch on the beach of that fierce light. Hand scribe the sign HC SVNT DRACONES (our own quietus a land so far it can't be seen). Turning everything that is dark into devouring white?

II

Beyond all those habitations of middle dimensions, ghosts hover and congregate. Shadowy, insubstantial. On roads, against walls of buildings, they appear and disappear. A pattern, a wave, moving in and out of the present. Unstable. Featureless. Unruly. Searching. Looking for us. On freezing rain swept streets we feel the cold draught of their passing.

***

Our fathers fought in the desert, for an obsolete empire. Year after year, chasing the shadow of an elusive enemy. His campfires and his middens buried. Each day the wind shifted the terrain so that the way forward became the way by which they arrived. Puzzled. Dazzled by sun glare. Beset by mirages. Their maps useless. They wandered for years amid plundered mosaics and the ruined temples of former empires. Watching the stars. Listening in the night wind to the approach of imaginary armies.

***

Nightly in the dark alcove we sit, listening. To a name that is intrinsically restless, inherently absent. To a dark energy unadorned by substance. In the silence curating our collection of perdurable objects, glass cabinets frantically rattling as an open door lets in the wind.

***

What false Arcadia at the sill still beckons? We were warned but we went on, with our empty pilgrimages, our spoiled wine, to the glacier's foot. Having chosen, all along, the wrong route. Our oarlocks rusted. Our rudder half sheared off. Unaware each destination alters with each new trajectory from which it is approached.

***

And Alexander (that footloose traveller) of Macedon's illustrious tutor had, amongst many, one curious shortcoming. He conducted himself "as if he were analysing things and not ideas."

***

Under the oar's heave the pull and pluck of longing. That vast and dim interior, deep within the sea's disorder, in which the mind magnifies itself, and is extinguished. There is no end to it. And no beginning

***

Dust on those guano islands and their reefs. On the exhausted seas about them. On that "City Beautiful. The White City" with "little brown men ... who look like rats" and other exotic exhibits "blacker than buried midnight". Dust on the broken basilica knee deep in rubble. On the dowdy tear stained dais from which the actors still are leaving. Dust on the thousand irradiated quays and their goodbyes. On all the buntinged gangplanks rising after having performed their perfect obeisance to the shore.

***

At the gate and at the window, ideal outline of an ideal object. Conflations of sense perceptions. Episodes of mind. Point us toward an empty room. A bare space where there are no formations.

***

Looking into that white plume, that blossoming white-hot cloud of darkness, of nothing.

Unsubdued Singing

"The Absolute has no history"
F.H. Bradley

I

They left no footprints in the sand when they were leaving. Light footed as ghosts they drifted with their possessions over the dark waterways and sluices. Saying not a word to each other. Into the fading light they departed.

***

The land they laid bare they left behind them. Scorched rock. Embers. Corpses along the wayside and in the orchards. Contaminated water. What was the land to them? And the people? A staging ground, merely, for their adventures.

II

A delirium of spent images. Placing the eucharist of what they consumed, and what consumed them, on the tongue. A word, a thing. There was no difference. A liturgy of empty sound. Rubbing the little stone idol at the masthead. Delivering prayers in the fo'c'sle. To imbue with shape all that flotsam of drifting sense. Past white capped rocks on furious isthmuses. To restrain the incubus. Enshrine an order.

***

To have seized, in that delirium, the path to an unexplored evening heavy with scent of pine, where air held a long looked for confirmation of why they set out. Sure footed amid snares. Clearing their way over revetments and roads of bone. Expropriators of a gaze, *Oculus Mundi*, fixed steadily upon stars, upon all their awkward alignments and conjunctions, guiding hand and mind through obscure waters. Weighed down with soteriological cargoes. With that ideal order to which the present adverts. Interdicting the return.

***

Standing in the fragrant pharmacopoeia of the future. "History is more or less bunk … We don't need [it]" Breathing a pure air. Of epaulets ("nailed into naked shoulders") and instantiations. Man, rigid as a gnomon, issuing orders. Paradisial vapours wafting across a lawn. Enveloping a flagstaff. Stiffly saluted.

III

Dissolved moment. Unnavigable sensum. On the long road that stretches from it an eternity of longing. An unexculpated journey. Hymn to the not moving. How History ignores the moment. Compiling, instead, its aggregate of false clues. Its granary of composited diversions. Who, in fact, writes the history in which one believes one is living?

***

Broken amulets and broaches. Artefacts of a different order. Carbonised bone, hair and flesh. Trowel of a blunt archaeology. Unearthing nothing. Except, in those two fiercely irradiated cities, penumbras that might have been persons. Rather than 'savages', spent images for discarding.

***

Heading into death lands. Cold dark points of a far north that is always calling. Beneath bright summer foliage. Hand moving the curtain. Implicate, always, in each border one constructs round object, act. Ordering, day in day out, the afternoon and the evening that will succeed one.

IV

There, where there was no longer any current, sea swell or wash of wave against them, they beheld, on the sand white littoral where the air with its fragrant exhalation had encalmed them, an unfamiliar spirit or apparition, walking out of the trees down to the water, a sprig of pine in its hand, beckoning to them to follow.

***

Sylvanus. In the deep wood: "salvages". "Veraye brute". A crying. A panick. Through pine groves, "extreame thicke". God give to us the order, they thought, and the serenity of a Garden.

***

Overgrown. In shadow. The mind is. To such a degree they could penetrate no further. Hugging the coast line. Fording the estuaries. The sound of birds all round them. An unsubdued singing. So tame they would have eaten out of their hands if they had food for them.

***

Scent of pine on the air. Sudorific. Of another order. Over everything yellow sulphurous waft of pollen. Ripple of night wind across river. Be-*wildered*. Without a path. To lose their way in "a wilderness" of unfamiliar signs and voices. Following artifice of compass, ruler. Into time's lost thickets and days. Into a different time, of day, of year. Of place. Unaware they were in it. That they had left that absolute order of their own.

***

Where swamp maple and dogwood are in bloom. Their petals adrift on abraded water. Dark, oleaginous green under banks. White, over the granite bed, scintillant at the centre. Incessant, migratory movement. Leaving no record of where it began. Or will end.

***

""I give to you a red road" … All [things] walking on the good red road together."

***

Over the bloodstained roads the voice of time. Beating the backwoods, searching the underbrush, the tangled roots round crumbling columns, for it. "Tempus Fugit". In the light of a day that is swiftly running away from itself. Into the cracked basin of the fountain on the lawn. Only to enter again, beyond the window overlooking them, the woods that are empty of it.

A Country Without Names

(2022)

In Memory of Campbell Matthews

***

"In the 1920s British cellist Beatrice Harrison began practicing outdoors [and] nightingales ... began matching her arpeggios with carefully timed trills ... getting used to her they ... burst into song whenever she began to play. In 1924 ... the BBC [recorded her in her garden]. The duet was repeated live each year ... In 1942 ... the recording engineer hearing the droning sound of the beginnings of the Thousand Bomber raid on Mannheim shut off the sound ... A strange soundscape of menacing bombers and incessant nightingales singing ... in the midst of human destruction and violence."
David Rothenberg   *Why Birds Sing*

***

Rock Star Celebrates Birthday at Exclusive Country House Retreat

Faint whiff of Grand Entrait, Clive Christian.
Beside the helipad, lake and gable-ivy ripple.
Subservient gravels crunch. The "proud, ambitious heap"
greets another well-heeled group. Round the inglenook
at dark babble of toasts under poster mock-up,
El Presidente, of birthday host. Looking down on
all the plunder, from Famagusta to Ferghana.
Finial, pediment, alabaster frieze: the frozen flight
from ennui. It's dead and scattered parts
cast in plaster, or bronze. A fixed expression
of a rapacious age. History narrating profit with loss.
Celebrity hedonists frolic amid its bric-a-brac.
Reluctant, atop their leafy sylvan slope, to engage
with what – head of walrus, polar bear, taxidermy
of arctic night – beyond all wealth, privilege
and power, might hold up before them
                              a reproving gaze.

Road to the North

> "Homeward you think we must be sailing
> to our own land."
>
> Homer   *Odyssey* [X: 538-539]

I

Suddenly at the end of day, spectral tree blown
against the window, my father appears before me, marching
leading a shabby contingent of ghosts. They pause,
and then, the sound of half empty canteens
slopping at their waists, approach. I watch them, as if
through a stirred-up haze of dust, fragments
from a broken century, their laughter
and song drifting, as they march,
through time's porous and permeable borders
into our own, dissolving all horizons
and distances, shedding the dead weight
of months and years, to appear before
me, reinvigorated. Ghosts, feeding on my blood.

II

I ask him how they managed to arrive, unscathed
out of that gloom at the world's end. "Although
we summoned ourselves" he said "we were loath to
come back, knowing the way, that it would hold for us
only professed guilt. But for pity of you, and to see you
once again and warn you, before the clouds of darkness
block, finally, any hope of return ... On the way
by which we came, city after city, nothing but a heap
of smouldering stones, smoke, soot strewn mosques,
hospitals, bodies piled up on pavements, waiting.
As if entire countrysides and cities had been
offered up as burnt sacrifices to the god Mithra,
their odours pleasing to him. An ancient temple to him
preserved, parts of it, in the basement of the House
of Finance which, as we came closer to you,
we saw rising, all steel and glass, like a lance head
flashing under cloud, tilting at the very heavens
themselves. And all around us at night FIRE
the sleepers in untold doorways and hauling,
during day, bags stuffed with their possessions
from bench to low wall to under a bridge
out of the rain. Like those groups of vagabonds
listlessly adrift roaming the turnpikes after their land
was seized, their towns pulled down about their ears,
centuries ago. Home is always the testing ground for
cruelties we later export. In fading light we heard
the clank of uncoupled cars in the goods yards and,
from them, a low and muffled tune of despair. Its refrain
rang in our ears, hour after hour..."

III

He went on, measuring, carefully, his words: "Conscience,
as we set out, compelled us to re-visit the very places
where we had inflicted so much pain on others; not to
relinquish to forgetfulness, by one ounce, the weight of
our degeneracy. And to show you, in one broad sweep,
both your inheritance and our burden. So we began
where experience first indicted us … Exhausted by heat,
some apoplectic, we dropped like flies by the roadside,
where they buried us. Our cemeteries marched with us,
boon companions. Incised in stone, nameless –
most too low in rank to warrant more than 'private soldier' –
we were left behind; no loved ones who would come
grieving for us later, on that road to the north,
Uttarapath they call it, would be able to find where
we lay. Wormsmeat. Slowly ingested and excreted;
our boots laid with us in that night in case we might
rise up and take again to walking…" And I thought
I caught on the air, for one instant, the smell of
stale sweat and moist leather, of scorching dust.

IV

Noticing the torn and scrofulous uppers
of their boots, I pitied them; that, stirring out of Erebus,
they'd had to traverse its smoke-filled chasms of
vaporous, blood-soaked roads to reach us. "My son" he said
"one need go no further than the nearest manhole and
pry off its lid, to let the fistula's dark stream that's
always under your feet, its rustling skin of vapours,
escape: here; where lies are roared out loud, where
the deepest vein of villainy is silence. The majority,
disdaining the stench, slam back the lid at once.
Few dare to linger over what so deeply offends
their sense of who they are: saviour or destroyer?
We are not, my son, what we so flatteringly imagine
ourselves to be. But comfort makes cowards of us all.
Let us continue, then, our blighted wanderings
so you may better grasp our burden, your inheritance…"

V

"At the edge of desert steppe were groves of date palms.
Dates and dung we called it: the camp. D and D. Knee deep
in dates. And camel dung: some rolled their cigarettes from it.
Little did we know what was to come. And in the evenings we fell
about to yarning about our days together on the Grand Trunk
Road. Said we remembered most the smells of spices and
incense intertwined with dust. Not that they weren't present
where we were. But less intense, varied. Remembered the
wayside shrines brightly bedecked, athrong with people. All that
colour, farrago of activity. And then the stillness, and the
silence after, in shadow under the banyan. A doze at midday,
when the sun was at its highest. Them – not us. Our boots
marching, always marching. And the dhaba, the road-side eateries.
Flatbreads crisping over coals. And onward it went, over fifteen
hundred miles, broad and smiling. Old hands from those parts,
with a smattering of Hindi, waxed lyrical (ah, nostalgia, it is a
dish one never tires of eating) about the coasts,
port-cities where their fathers settled and traded. Where,
bunnias told them, even the parrots once spoke in five languages
when the trade routes were open and flourished. But
where, last century, when our presence became too much
of a burden to them, all that remained were soot blackened
burnt out bungalows and stations. And then gallows.
Lynchings that went on for years. Every 'nigger' (one old hand
mimicked the distress on the bunnia's face) they came
across strung up. Shot. Or bayoneted. Man. Woman. Child…"

VI

"Years later, chest deep in water, waiting
for the small boats to ferry us, ranged out
along the shore, all I could think of was sand
and the abandoned roads which, after we'd
disembarked at Haifa, ran off into it,
the settlements and villages which we pulled
down without compunction. And those we left
standing, bereft, without a home or food
or means of subsistence, in their own country."
His eyes lowered upon his hands, as if suddenly
they had become the seat of all impurity,
transgression, and stayed there a long time, even
after he resumed talking. "And even later still,
many years on, after we had left that cold, grey
northern coast, re-posted to another, warmer
country, in their eyes whenever they met ours,
in their pained look of scrutiny, I was reminded." Again
he stopped, again looked at his hands. "Of what?"
I asked. "Of fear. In our own. That went
unacknowledged. Of the order, months later,
to burn. Burn all the crates. So many of them.
Crammed with files. And to rake, and re-rake, all
the waste, reduced, already, to ash. And to make
sure nothing of it survived that was not
"broken up". Fear. Theirs, that gave the order.
And ours. In a crateful of ash. So desperate
to extinguish what, in all those records of
organised violence and inhumanity, proved us inferior
to those we slanderously depicted as inferior
to ourselves. Fear. Of exposure, and of obloquy…"

VII

Another of the regiment, flaxen haired, still with the
cloud of an untimely death about him, who,
with my father, had survived to reach the beaches
where they stood waiting to be taken off, but who,
weakened by fatigue and cold, had drowned before
they could haul him aboard, spoke, in a lifting Antrim
accent: "We were, like someone wrote, no more
than uniformed assassins. Nothing we, or our leaders,
did could atone for the misery we'd inflicted
on so many innocent of any crime but trying to live
in their own country ruled by their own kind.
Fleeing, later, through the city where most of us
would eventually embark, I stumbled onto the black
cobblestones, tripped by a fallen wire. All the
telegraph lines were down. Your father helped
me up and I limped off, half walking/trotting
and looking frequently back for any sign of the
pursuer who, at that very moment, was doing no more,
or less, than we had for untold years been doing –
crossing the borders of a sovereign country in force
to take and claim it as our own. And in some cases,
where they wouldn't put up with it, exterminating
them." He shivered. Then shuffled. Tugged his collar
up … "In truth", my father concurred "it could be said
that before we were the victims of those who
pursued us, we were their accomplices, preparing
the ground for the horrors that were to come…"

VIII

At first light I saw my father's figure at the window
against the stirring undulations of lace, wavering,
bending with them from a breeze out of darkest
Erebus, and shedding that semblance of solidity
it had retained for the journey to us. As I moved
towards him his form stabilised. I drew back.
"We'll soon be gone" he said. "Here, fear bred out of greed,
bred out of loss of trust, urged us, dead spirits, back. 'Thieves
and liars' we were called, when living. Justly. For that
our souls daily scald, simmer on burning sand, on live
coals." The window rattled to a violent gust, pushing
the pane in then drawing it back. "Put no faith in good
works. They only paper over cracks. It's here", pointing to
his chest, "work's done. Here alone. Trust no one's word.
But when they act, weigh stated intent with consequence
– to see if they are one. That way you'll drive out the rat
beneath the pile. A lifetime's work. You'll get
little help. Good luck … Here, from what we've seen,
perjury, in all spheres of public life, is not a crime.
So with the law at large, home and abroad. Ignored.
Bent. Or remade. To fit the purposes of the rich, the
powerful … The day after they wrenched that flagstaff from
the lawn in front of Government House, sweating and silently
cursing, they merely thrust and planted it in another
land. Later, in another form. Right through the heart.
Masters of deception. Their trade. From 'Empire' to
'Commonwealth'. Mere name-change: "To smell
much sweeter in the public nose." But, at the end of day,
the only ones such trade truly benefits are their own…"

IX

"Here all the oracles have fallen silent.
All the shrines, and their *genius loci*, have
been abandoned. All the observances,
the oblations. All ancient ritual,
supervising terror. The desert's getting
nearer and nearer." I watched my father as he
pondered us. Alienated sojourners. Worshippers
of false idols. He saw us, clandestinely
nurtured by a state intent on preventing us
identifying common purpose, straying out of
our dried-up paths into ruinous ideological
postures. Narrow doctrinal, sentimental
utopias of political propriety. Thirsters
whom the thirst disfigures, distorts.
On our city walls and our street corners
he saw only the graffiti of a corrupted
faith. After he left I dreamed I saw him, and
his shabby contingent, again, walking
through the twilight dust of Uttarapath,
as if they were walking through a sacred
grove, far from what they'd experienced
here: rubble and spolia. Our chthonic
shrines long since dismantled and buried
beneath a network of motorways and malls.

X

In the dead of winter, now, I return, to the
pitted granite of his headstone, tilting
on the small bluff above the river, as if
blown crooked by the wind which always blows
here. Beneath me, through thin aspen and alder,
the dust of a suburban Sahara moves on the air
above shallow marsh embankments, darkening
against the edge of a sky grey as that half-
light moving up out of the river, and I know
there will not be another nekuia, that
"[we] will never find that life for which
[we] are looking." A drowsy congregation,
laity of restless consumers, easily distracted
by each latest invention; deferential, mindlessly
concordant with our "sowre complexion[ed]" clergy
in its towers of steel and glass, rising
above us. Victims of a corrosive insecurity,
we sail off into the future never looking
back; unable to ascertain, alienated
from repetition, a rhythm, a pattern, a music
woven into the air and the earth and
heart which beats in accordance with it.

Alder

"'Everything is eternal, yet nothing is constant.' The entire landscape... is a nexus of Power moving beneath the outward appearance of things ... of Persons shifting in and out of form, of patterns recombining."

Ruth Holmes Whitehead *Mi'kmaw Legends*

I

That look in each other's eye. Brief
moment of terror. Foreboding.
On the road we did not follow.
In the field we did not plough.
At the quay from which we never departed

Instead of assarts, palisadings:
the dust-filled spoor, the chewed stem.
Interpreting the sign. In the night
the sound of our fire in the wind.
An ember, a bone. Cracking.

Pale blossoms trickling our faces.
Feathering air. Listening to names.
Of those who wandered off into towns
and cities. Those who did not return.

II

Branch against branch.
Squeaking. In wind round
the fire at night. Rubbing.
Or is it the longspur, again,
in the deep wood, calling?

A cold wind screams
through the emptiness
of asylums. From far off.
We hear it. In the snow
that is falling. We cannot
make out our breath.
Or the tracks of
the animals that
           are leaving.

What if we should arrive in a place
we have not been in before.
A place whose guardians we
might have offended. Bearing,
in our arms, no gifts
of conciliation. Searching,
under drifts, for last year's shoots.
Listening. For a pattern, a rhythm?

At night, in the deep wood.
At year end. In the dark. Chanting.
Alder. Bear's blood. Sap
of the ministrating moon.
A circuit. In the roots
the figure of a man. Breathing.

III

That song. Heard once deep
in the wood. Not forgotten.
Celebrating. *Something must
leave for something to return.*
To hold the breath, as security,
for a perpetual bequest. For
the re-turns flesh rejoices in.

Where nothing, beyond the
staked out boundary, seems
to be what it appears to be.
Like smoke, in and out
of branches. Vestment,
of many unfoldings. Pausing.
Coming and going. A trail,
with signs on it. Fragrant
with possibility.
                    We walk on it.

Scent of dry grass, scorched dust.
Silence sifted. Tenuous note.
Weaving through branches. Heard,
and not followed. Followed
and lost. To where night leads.
In shadow. Eater and eaten.
Surmounting terror. In solvents
of the long dawn that follows.
      Touch.

IV

Tracks of Ursus, in the cold
night sky above us. Crunch
of snow in the deep wood.
Crack of frozen branches.
Prey and pursuer, in an
imperishable pattern, wheeling
on their axis. Above the ebb
and flow and tumult endless
ly spread out beneath them.

One night, after many nights, in a wild place
amid sunken roots and sounds, of scattered shapes
and shadows, alone, and wrestling with phantoms
the marching minute hand of time, a fool's errand
and burden, cutting out shapes from nothing
to do its bidding, fell away and I could hear,
through rustling foliage, smell and see at last,
beneath that fluid vestment of its being
in which it had been cast, one part bear and

one part person, the vision move toward me.
That other shape and dwelling in which my own
shape could not last, overwhelmed and then,
as earth inhales and exhales our shadow,
released me. Seven nights it came, with a gentle
rustling of foliage, to where I lay or sat.
And stopped and looked for a long time at me.
Its gaze inquisitive, penetrating. And then I knew,
at almost its last visit, what it was thinking:
'So you too would wear the clothes of a bear. And I,
too, in them, could come and sit beside your fire.
And neither you, nor I, would let the other go hungry'.

Through cold taut air we look up
under a canopy of startled stars.
The Great Bear above us, at
the still centre of the revolving
world. Moves, pivots through
the night sky and, again, we follow.

In the deep shadow under the tree.
In the rubble of scattered stones,
bits of bark and earth, within it.
Known, but not heard. Heard, but not
seen. In fragments of birdsong.
All day. All night. Arising. Because
each thing is, in some way, united.
Within the shadow of the tree. Moving.
Amongst the living and the dead.

Envoys and emissaries. Of
an indestructible energy. Gained
and spent, transferred and
assimilated, dissipated. Only,
again, to be renewed. Elusive
divinities, circling us round the fire
at night. Circling, in a never
ending inhalation, exhalation.
Keeping it going. A rhythm,
                        a pattern.

And those who breathe, in
the shadow. Wait. Hold back.
In the flickering half-light.
Understand. Terror in their eyes.
The Forms. The passing procession.
Then raise their voices. Chanting.
At year end. Under the alders.
                    Keeping it going.

V

In the deep wood, all day long,
the call of the longspur. But
fewer and fewer of us each
year, many wandering off into
towns and cities, to hear it.

Only a cold wind through
the trees. Only the wind
shaking boughs, weaving
through far off asylums,
through empty lots and
run down malls. And the rain.

Driven Dust

[*Some surviving fragments from an unofficial account recorded by a temple scribe at Uruk during the reign of Rim-Anum. It consists of observations by a man captured in a military campaign to procure corvée labour from amongst 'unadministered' gathering hunting and fishing communities south of Uruk.*]

"O the folly of you who follow each day the furrow, knee deep in milk, semen and dung, sweating in the dark byre. Hacking the rock face. In the deep tunnel. Or tethered for months upon plains, bitten by black fly, counting (#3)

Constructors of storage pits, grain houses you dream under a starless roof. Proclaimers of omens and auguries, always genuflecting, praying, organising offerings. Anxiously measuring hours, days. Your calendars do not console you. (#5)

By eating your fear you do not rid yourselves of it. At your shrines where sacrifices are performed, in your lavishly wrought Hall of Administrators, you confirm and endorse it. Then manipulate and, for your own profit, exploit it. (#11)

You look down on us. 'You're driven dust: over the hills and through the trees, creeks and marshes' you say. 'Children. Never settling in one place long enough. Drinkers of unclean water.'" (#8)

Where No Snow Falls

"Rosy-fingered Dawn has broken her coloured pencils. Now they lie
scattered about like nestlings with empty, gaping beaks."

Osip Mandelstam *The Egyptian Stamp*

It was clear to their companions
before they left, from ominous mutterings
about 'this bordello of a world',
that their journey was not to
extend love, or understanding.
But to gratify avarice. A boy's dream.
To arrogate dominion, practice cruelty.

Headstrong, they were unable
to restrain them from leaving.
For coasts where scent of cedar
carried many miles out to sea
to them. For shores where charcoal
burners waited, their fires raising
dark clouds turning noon into night:
where apparitions appeared before
them, phalloi round their necks,
striding with outstretched arms.

Under a brine damp bluff.
Embers of logs. Charred bones
of offerings. Spilled lustral water.
Wine. On the beach, beside the quay,
dark stain of caulking. As they departed
they called out to those on the shore:
"We are the voice of Man apart.
We speak the language,
the triumphant tongue, of History."

*Those who stand, the dispossessed,
by the roadside. Abayas fraying beneath
loads. In driving sand. Sun glare.
Clutching pots and pans. Listening
to far off explosions. Neither forgotten.
Nor acknowledged. Live on, in the black
wind at the horizon. In a broken-
floored orphanage. Beside a rusting
swing. Gate with hinges twisted.*

Above salt-caked tholepins
dead bird pinned in a forestay
its cries unheard. In thresh of wind's fury.
In wave surge, counter-surge.
"The land where no snow falls,
nor long frost of winter." On slithery
benches. Recited, over and over.
Amidst loosening breakers.
Embroidered on each foaming ridge.

Endless, sea-choked divagations.
Skins salt, wind scoured.
Days and nights outlasting
tempests. Hauled, to the
precipice's edge. Dropped. Years.
Thinking. Back to an old quay
by a fleece-scrub headland
and a glorious welcome. Cool
shade of laurel at the well. Sweet
smell of broom. Sound of
woodpecker in copse of hazel.

Others in leaking boats,
wash up on perilous reefs.
Or in the deep sea, wallowing.
Overcrowded. Young and old.
Fleeing each decimated village.
With little water. Less food.
Requesting sanctuary. Their cities
in flames. Some drowning
in sight of those same lands
from which the despoilers
                            had set out.

Mid-day heat: desiccated air.
Dust. Chirr of cicada. On the
deeply wooded ascent slow sound
like water. Breeze rippling
leaves. On the bleached track
no footprint. Beside a grey clump
of olive trees, high on a scarp
of crumbled rock, they located
the shrine, and the oracle…
'To have climbed this far
is to have mistaken the sound
of longing for the sound of water.
For what you would quench
you need not have travelled so far'

Reliquary

(For James Hamilton-Paterson)

"He who has gone beyond ... who
has crossed to the other shore."
Dhammapada [26: 414]

Nameless land. Haunting the salt marsh
and the ridges above it. Where
my childhood is a shimmering chip
washed from the stream's bed.
A latent pattern, a tendency. But
no point of rest. No permanent object.

To carry sorrow with one. From the very
beginning. On the worn trackway. From
the moss boughed orchard's proffered vowels.
Through cuttings of wounded field maple.
To
        the sound of fracture.
        Of necessary distance.

And the light said: "There is no necessary distance. To follow the teloi in the stream's bed, anticipate nothing. Listen to birds call above the silted wharf, its timbers cracked and rotting. Can you discern from their flight where desire and goal co-incide?"

To negotiate, always, a modified terrain.
To refuse the words. To break the circuit
of appropriation. So the pattern falters.
                              Only to be re-traced.
In the ordinary conversation. Indicating
a point of reference. Concealing
                     a necessary silence.

Mossed boughs move in wind
through a sediment of syllables.
Of projected attributes, fears, needs.
Our universal categories. Perfecting
a man, woman. And the stream seeps
into the parched ground at their feet
like a stain. Carrying them forward.

But the sorrow remained:
on the faded trackway,
strewn with blossom, a way of ancient
conciliatory voices. Unobscured under
the weight of their intoning.

At the edge of water.
When leaves were falling.
After the first insults,
    woundings.
Air hardened.
    Light faltered.
In the unbroken circuit.
The world doubled.

And the pattern persisted. Daily.
In thousands of 'disownings', appropriations.
Until the necessary feint was infolded,
included in the act. And the distance
became a mandatory deception.

*
* *
*

Washed from the stream's bed.
Shining white chip. My shadow
beside me. Into the broken world
of sound and sense. Into the tangled
maze nestled at the salt marsh's
edge. Inaudible. Invisible. Until in it.

Sound coveted. Sense commanding.
A systematic link. A pattern
between sound and meaning. Across
an infinite variety of sounds and meanings.
Supplanter, discreditor of silence.
Of that syntax of what can't be said.

In the orchard
    sound of a swing
moving in wind.
    Empty.
        Voices.
Moving among trees.
            "There
  is nothing,
apart from the expression,
  to be expressed."

    A swing.
  Moving. Moved.
     In wind.
Beyond you. Beyond
  all sound
        words.

   After the alteration
of air to accept what the ear,
assimilated in the pattern,
commended to your attention.
                        After
  the end of birdsong.
On the faded trackway by
the ashwood you heard,
      dance
  of leaf / dust,
in the shadows' dry
           asseveration,
   nothing.

*
* *
*

Under flowering dogwood. New-laid topsoils
held sediment of brick, beam. Reliquary
of plaster, wallpaper, bone. Debris of Doodlebug,
incendiary. Barges, heavy with it.
Past Shoreditch, Gravesend. Entering
the Lower Hope. Dim, charnel water
that the stream, from its sand-capped
scarp where you dangled feet, daily fed.

Into your cuff-frayed hand, snow wrapped,
a letter, indissoluble judgement handed down:
to an Inferior Person.
        Years later, recalling
job interviews, its repeated indictment.
In their ears a coarse-grained accent.
Assembly line future. Honorarium of ditches,
doffing. Plate full of
                cold potatoes.

Fracas outside the gates. Bludgeon
of wood to right femur. Blood
stained kerbstone, resistant
to erasure. Inside, after the bell had gone,
simmering quiescence. Touching of breast.
Trouser pocket of hardness. Subject
transformed,
                into hapless object.

Slowly, noiselessly over the years,
under the dogwood,
the drip and seep, through untold
strata. Drip and seep. Noiseless
  accruing.

*
* *
*

    Marsh marigold
        flowering rush,
   infiltrate
substitute themselves for
each object. By the ashwood,
on the trackway murmurous
with voices. The pattern
prevails, the circuit is
    unbroken.
              Always,
   a little further
a little more estranged
from where you are
from where the moment
   occurs, undiverted.

    Beneath the parched
   sand-scarp, by dried out
banks of silt, the wharf
timbers, quietly, are
    warping
            cracking.

But beneath the ridge, on that faded
trackway when the sound of the voices was
almost unheard above the shift of wind
through thin salt mists drifting northward
your shadow returned, beside the ashwood,
                              to remind you.

And the light said again: "Anticipate nothing."
On a gatepost a bird sang.
And, for a moment, the pattern was
interrupted. In the silence that ensued
there was another, deeper, silence
                              haunting the ridges.
Without which you could not proceed.

   At the heart
of the dis-continuous present
the sensation (verbally silent)
 of birdsong
  not birdsong itself

that which could not
  be heard:
    name   letter
      mouth
   ful only   of a
                       ir

*
* *
*

In the orchard, where you left
your name incised in bark. In
each honeyed vowel. In the mossed
sediment of syllables upon
each branch, their accrued
appetencies, the weight of darkness
and sweetness. There the swing moves,
still, of its own accord. Empty.
In a wind emptied. Full
                        of silence.

Midsummer fires along the ridge
where you wandered, a pebble
from the stream's bed in your palm,
warming what once was molten
turning it over and over.
Memory of fire. Bright flicker
of water, flame. Fused
                        brick
    and bone.

Apple blossom, leaf
   air fragrant
with them,
     the sound of sense
         ripening
  on the tongue,
    consume
and console what,
   ultimately, cannot
  ever return
         to what was
apple blossom

     l
      e
   a
      f

      Drip
        of dew
   from the tall blades
      of grasses
at the salt marsh's edge.
    In the stillness
     which moves
out across sea embankments.
  In the unexpiated light
     which drains
from the estuary's mouth.
       Drip.

Drip.

*
* *
*

At sand-capped scarp
stream hard as glass
                        snow
piled high on trackway
bereft of voices, on
the quiet inlet below.

          A lone figure
  on the shore:
motionless, in a place erased
of mark or sign, white
as snow continually falling
straining to look
             to the further shore.

Uncomfortably at Home
(*IM* Randal Bingley)

Out of their broken shadows they emerge
trees, much as they were, fixed years ago
in a sepia image of this Thameside village.
I stand on its descending road, where
in 1381 Tomas Baker ignited a countrywide
rebellion attacking poll-tax commissioners
collecting revenue for more foreign wars.
Liberally, richly festooned now with litter
of a nation hopelessly addicted to endless
consumption. Swept clean each day by
an array of cleaners, remunerated by
a state grown wealthy from centuries
looting overseas possessions. Where
the road ends at an earthen sea-wall
a sailing-barge sits, still, on a sepia evening
in 1909, on or off-loading at high water
in the lay-by of a wharf now vanished.

The trees shake down on me a dusty
pallor: consequence of that moment
standing when young before for the
first time the strange swaying motion of
their beauty. Wanting, but being unable,
to surrender to it. To trees, tideway and
village: habitat of one who, bereft
of qualifications, felt trapped beside a tidal
waste, targeted as raw material, provider of
surplus. A feeling that festered. Leading me
to put thousands of miles between it and
myself. Metic, for decades, under tropical sun.
No longer sucked down among a class content

to sink not swim, kept docile with a few stale
tidbits, a day off each week, an employer's
annual seaside outing, while in Westminster
they gulped subsidised wine and meat.
And what if I'd remained, instead, at home
looking out over the dammed-off navigable
tideway that had effected an entrance to the
village once, amid those trees, and people
many whose names, not faces, I have forgotten,
and so much else, in this country whose
history, so much of it, happened overseas?
But to have returned, to have become
domesticated once more to the violence
of that history, of its ruinous expropriations
overthrowing of governments, torture
pauperisation and death, would have been
                            not to have left at all.

On a raw December evening shadows
sweep into a dusty stand of trees
topping the bluff, rattling churchyard gate
dimming headstone inscriptions of family,
pilots who traversed these treacherous tidal
flats, and I hear, immobilised within a maze
of mud and water, their sighs. They echo
along channels. Over embankments guiding
the inlet's flow where I've wandered mind
navigating an endless historical discourse
of incorporation and exclusion, corroborating
neither. Under trees, now, I stand beside a leafless
road and pick a stray white hair from my collar.
Then turn my head out of the wind that blows
across the long grey waste of channels.
In the autumn air a presentiment of snow.

Road of Dust

"The north wind rolls the white grasses and breaks them."
Ts'en Ts'an

I

Deep red, still, leaves in winter. Edged
white with frost. By the stone pond in the east
courtyard. They chitter, stiff as husks, in
the wind. Within it the stink of blood.
By the south wall the willows are grieving.
Corpses pile up in alleys and on streets.
No one has the strength to bury them.
A bushel of rice now fetches ten thousand
copper coins. In the dead of night the sound
of rats rummaging. Of owls, hunting.

II

Beside Clear Mind Pavilion wind
blows cold. Over terraces of jasper
balustrades of marble, in the east
courtyard. Over all accumulations of
successively disappearing
moments onto which we hold. Extinguishing
fires of inured appetency. I listen.
To silence. To the chanting of
sutras over the lichened steps
under the eaves as we depart, at day-
break. Pale smoke of wild cherry blossom
hovers on trees in the courtyard.

III

The journey north. Digesting hard roads.
Admonished, stoking factional
deliberations, by our griefs. Surprised.
In the wheel's smouldering nave, on
the dust-thronged axletree, we hear
the smoking world revolve. The crack
of it, day after day, in each ice-dark rut.
Its iron rim sinking. Then rising. And
the flutter and quivering rasp, in the cob's
nose and mouth, of air. Caught in its mane
a cloud of spangled sweat is freezing.

IV

At the Mingde Gate wind blows
cold. And colder. We wait. The folds
of our garments stiffen. Words
in our mouths grow heavy with the weight
of surrender. In a white line beneath
the persimmon trees – attired as if for a
funeral. We shiver. Biding his time,
with a long retinue of retainers,
languidly, Taizu drifts toward us. Uncouth,
with an imperious gaze, and no ear
for music. Except the disorganized sound
of battle. Behind him, in weak winter light,
gleam of deep azure finials. I run
my tongue around my mouth, trying to dispel
sourness of weeks of incarceration.

V

Voices of bargemen from the canal:
poling and exhorting as, slowly, with a
cargo of salt from the coast, they pass.
Sounds from teahouses and carriages
thread streets of the south quarter. Peddlers
hawk quinces beside the outer courtyard.
I shut my eyes in early morning glare.
Mind drifts. Shadows of marble and jasper
float. Broken. Sifted. A stream: of
accumulations. Of name and form. "The world
is only names". A corvée trudges to the canal
to dredge and haul till dusk all its dark filth.
The smell of it will hang for days on the air
filling the inner courtyard and rooms.

VI

Alone at the end of day. I lean on
the balcony gazing south, in dust that's
whirled from the dried out floodplain.
It stings my eyes. To my many titles now
Taizu has added another. Marquis of Wei
Ming: of Disobeyed Edicts. To tighten
the knot of my humiliation. In twelve
months: mother: milk-son: wife. Gone.
New, young wife, forced to his pleasure.
All night unable to sleep: across the
courtyard incense silently drifts
coiling, rippling blue scarves.
And a bulbul, hearing the smoking
world revolve, sings in the abandoned temple
overhung with willows beside the canal.

VII

From an imbroglio of dust and wind
in the inner courtyard, suddenly,
there came a faint and acrid smell,
like that of fish staled in warp
and weft of clothing. A man. Walking
out of the shadows. With a dirt stained
face, shouldering a basket. Zheng Wenbao.
Disguised. Last seen months before
by the stone pond in the east courtyard
where we had gathered. And then, in the
time it seems to take a gust of
wind to rise and pass, he was
gone. But from the long interlude
of our conversation, his astute eye
and speech penetrating the depths
of my condition, lodged in my mind, stayed,
his words: "Forget Jinling".

VIII

Amid unfamiliar smells, shapes, this
far north: shadows lengthen, deepen.
On the wind, for a moment, sounds
like chanted sutras. The bulbul
sings again from the ruined temple.
At all the river crossings, in my sleep,
the dead raise their heads. More
than a hundred thousand. In mud
their banners rot. Shrouds for hungry
orphans, widows. By the east courtyard
they lingered. Or flocking like phantoms
to the road, collapsed: too weak to

continue. Listening, there, to the smoking world revolve. Deep in its iron groove. And the scent of wild cherry blossom overflowed the east courtyard.

Under Jiu-yi Shan

"I now state my terms to the crocodiles. I set them a limit of three days to take their ugly selves south to the sea ... Do not repent when it is too late!"

    Han Yu   *Address to the Crocodiles of Chaozhou*

I

By the east lake the wind blows hard.
Over reed marsh, mud flat and shallow.
Tundra swan, stork and crane already
have landed. Out of that far barbarian
heaven where snow falls and falls without
stopping. Where, leaving, day after day they heard
nothing but the sound of wind through passes,
across ice-locked rivers, sweeping
the slightest hint of warmth before it.
At the lake edge I stand. Listening. Sedge, crisp
with frost, under my feet crunches. Wondering
at how winter has arrived so early.

II

On Great Marsh of Cloud Dream, alone,
I compose verses, to which no one will listen.
The court of Chu puff themselves up,
parade around, bristle. Idle and poisonous
chatter is all they engage in: a quagmire
of lies, vilifications and distortions
discrediting those who seek to curtail
their orgies of nepotism and licence.
They would, if they had to,
fill a bag of flowers with excrement
and proclaim that it smells fragrant.

They'd rather, I am sure, that I obliged
by falling into a river full of crocodiles
than ever reappearing amongst them. On
Great Marsh of Cloud Dream I chant
and the birds accompany me, migrants
from far lands, in a music of impending chaos.

III

Mist rolls in over muddy flag filled bottoms.
A rufous sandstone cloud erupts
from the lake's bed, when the foot's
thrust in it. A darkening pandemonium.
Beside me sweet caneflower-
silvergrass leans and shivers. Cold
October air. Wisps linger and curl
over long silt-spits that glisten half submerged.
From creek-head to creek-head the sound
of rites. Drumming. Drumming.
Unabated. Each nubile waist
encircled by an arm. Dancing and
pursuing in flux and twist of air and
water the whirlwind and the storm. To ease
the dried out heart. To atone. Old
crocodile skin, stretched under the
hand, whose broken lachrymose fate
is conjured and elucidated in your note?

IV

Eaten under the shade of
Jiu-yi Shan, in dark water
close to Burned Field Village.

At the placid, lapping margin.
So completely devoured, no sign
of them remaining. In each loose-reign
prefecture I ride through, carts loaded.
Families adrift on the roads. Sour
smelling, brackish the taste of a life
lived under Jiu-yi Shan. Far out
the sound of a storm brews over the water.
Muffled, intermittent rumbling.
I listen. Leaves of the orchid
tremble. Fleabane glimmers at the water's
edge, damp from a low cloud that hangs
heavily above it. In the air, scent
of cassia. Over the south running channels.
I point my horse's head toward them.
With a stumble, and a sigh, we follow.

V

Within a charred circle of thoroughwort
ash of incense and powdered bone.
Impress of makeshift shrine, dismantled.
Cloud black over vastness of water sky all
the way back to Ying. The damp wind spawns
sinister phantoms that writhe and twist
their way into the heart, when one is
not looking. Sinuous as guts of sacrifice
spread out and interpreted. But who
is the one who yields the life, and the
one who takes it? The sanctimonious cant
of those who thrive, courtiers covetous
of their own comfort and security, only drives the
knife deeper. I came upon this bloodstained
spot at evening, my horse exhausted

my stomach cramped with hunger, long after
the rites had ended. Behind me
from scattered bivouacs of those from
Chu who'd fled, rather than remain to see
the coming disaster, smoke was rising.

VI

The Imperial Inquisitors of Chin, a country
of wolves and tigers, sit in their gold
plated palanquins and dispense
injustice. Connoisseurs of terror their fingers whiten
often. No room for treatises on music,
philosophy or history in the Imperial
Archive. They burn them. And no need
to bury your head in the sand – they
will, if you write or read such nonsense,
do it for you. Or get someone else to:
there's never any shortage of hoodlums
among us. Each night paranoia stalks their bed-
chambers. Informers in every household. Too
many to unmask: who would unmask them?
When the wind blows south, over the
Han River, it is full of black dust.
Cities, townships and villages. Burning.
Slowly, it filters down upon us.

VII

Waste of protectorates, of vassals.
North of the Han River. A cold wind
cracks the faces, tears the banners of
Chin armies. But still they move south

ward devouring, like a silk worm, leaf
upon leaf. Massing on our borders.
Pretending it is we who are threatening
theirs. What can't be expropriated
by force they expropriate by trickery and
deception. Chin Shih Huang-ti, face of
jackal breast of bird of prey, has torn off
the cankered flesh of our court, bit by bit.
Gnawed through its heart. So easy to destroy
such credulous self-flattering fops
trading gold and precious stones for enslavement
to a corrupt bureaucracy of sycophants
willing to do anything for advancement.
So it has been since ancient times. Why
do I complain that men are blind today?
Jin Shang, Cheng Hsiu, Tzu Lan. May
you consume what you have harvested.

VIII

All the fragrant leaves have withered.
Orchid, sun-apple, white rumex, cart-halting
flower, sweet spirit grass. Fleabane bends
back in the wind. Over the muddy bottom
under Jiu-yi Shan my reflection wavers.
Words, like stones, sink. On the air strange accents.
From far prefectures northward. From a
government geared for war, not peace: women tilling
fields, men away expanding borders. Outlaws
in the forests and marshes. I raise my head.
A faint drumming over dark waves. The wind
blows hard. Cold hands lift cold water to
parched lips. White as thistledown my breath.
Suddenly all the birds are leaving.

A Country without Names

"To whom there are no accumulations, who have comprehended the nutriments, and whose range is the deliverance of the 'void' and 'signless' – their track is as hard to trace as that of birds in the sky"
Dhamapada [7: 92]

"And yesterday we will arrive"
he had said "in a country without names.
Where the past, decorated and mutilated,
will confront us on every street corner,
begging for alms and bread, veteran
of many wars and atrocities, coughing
in shop doorways at night, cold
with the stale sweat and weight of
a soiled historiography, cult of idols,
under its head. And nothing but a baleful
choir of cats and ghosts to sing it to sleep."

~~

Wisp of fragrance
on the air. Jasmine
or orange. As from
an unseen garden. Here
where they advanced,
crossing the narrow strait
wreathed in sea fog,
at the Western edge
of the world. Days,
long stretched out
to year end,
of carrion and blood.

Of dead gods. Their
names unrecited.

~~

        Broken,
    haunted ground.   All
previous moments   endure:
   afternoons devoured
by almanacs   uprooted gardens
   of shadows   smoke
     and blood
    flower again.
   A bird sings : the reality
of a single, unifying moment
                before words.
    Amid querulous
   apparitions
             days
  move.

~~

On the river, vapours tangle
ghostly rigging: bullion, gold plate,
coin. Undisturbed,
along with ensign and
corpse, buried. As we walk past
we hear, from houses
on the embankment

packed with benches, the rancid patter
of deodorized words. Abuzz
above a technology of extirpation.

~~

       Tumescence
of word on morning steps.
                      Rustle
of newsprint as we breathe
   in the air
         events
taking place around us. Near
   and far. It is only
background music. The sound
   of the times:
      a "polluted vehicle".
Day and night, it rolls over us.
   The voice, always,
of the revisable moment
   lost too soon,
        never
  recovered.
         Frozen
footprints on a lawn.
            A bird calling.

~~

Wisp of fragrance
on the air,
in the moonlit street,
as from
an unseen garden. There
memory moves,
     across

a waste expanse
of collapsed columns
statues, where
under motionless palms
     leaning
against fragments,
"actuated only by the
love of order and
justice" they "advance[ ]
towards perfection."

   ~~

  What did we see,
walking with our heads down,
beyond that gallery of "broken
statues and [...] tragic columns"
 assembled line of legends
  and heroes?
   In a state,
 from the very beginning,
of denial, the dead word,
 proposing everything
 & affirming nothing,
 pressed upon our tongue
  in a shadowy

consecration:
>   a counterfeit obolus
>   to ferry us across
>   the creaking river-ice
> to an embankment of buried
>   skulls and voices.

~~

Who "can change the attitude of
those with power [...] make himself heard?"
Through ruined orchards, in desolate
provinces, amid charred palms
fragments of staircases, scorched walls,
the chimera beckons: 'This way. This way.
Here there is gold, there is oil, there
is sugar, all manner of things we don't have,
or in insufficient quantity.' The moon

shines on sleeping forms in doorways.
As it always will. Those gods, their shrines
a fine dust on the antennae of cities, on
whom we might have called in a moment
of doubt, anticipating terror, have departed.
Leaving only, at blossoming sepulchres, dignitaries
bending the knee, adopting obligatory poses.

~~

    What are they for
               words
gods of an omnipotent country
on a station platform in winter
  reading the signs
            at a bank counter
calculating advantage and loss
or in the great clearing house
of the supramundane
              drawn
upon all of us
       sooner or later
  taken into account.

    ~~

    Birds cross the sky.
     Silent above
us as we lift our heads to watch
  them. They depart
 for a place unspecified
    undetermined.   A country
without names.
      Fleetingly
 their shadows write
on kerbstones at the corner of the street
where we stand. Our heads turn
   to follow a track
      we can only dimly
 make out. Returning again
  to where we stand.
           Foot
on kerb. Hand on familiar shoulder.

Listening.
To someone trying again to write
our history.
Trying to call the birds back.

White Fire

"Vain to listen to the love song which a ghost sadly sings"
Li Shang-Yin

    I

    In a seaside resort,
    bereft of family
    friends, a migrant
    from war-torn lands
    dreams of bunch grass
    in fierce light
    blowing before a door.
    A white fire.

    *

    Warm wind full of ghosts.
    Scent of lemon blossom.
    But no lemon blossom.
    Shadow land
    through which he walks
    meeting his shadow
    coming back.

    *

    At a cross roads
    amid spent bullet
    casings, discarded fan-
    belts and tyres
    someone is reciting
    a prayer
    and someone is crying

the name
of a town or village
to which they do not
know how to return.

*

Crepuscular forms
asleep in shop doorways
bus shelters.
Moved on.
Tumbleweed lives.
Trudging at dawn
past newsagent billboards
announcing more foreign wars.

*

A shadow moves
from ridge to ridge.
A dark fluttering
of birds. History
is what happens far
off. Across a lawn

onto patio steps
lilac scent drifts
on summer nights.

*

Warm wind full of ghosts.
One returns, always,
to a memory. A steppe
of ruined horizons.

Smoke. Dense,
drifting. At dusk, saltwort:
little pink flowers.
Rut and hummock.
And only bitter water to drink.

II

No shrapnel-severed dream
here. Just broken limbs
of trees after the storm, debris from
overturned bins of garbage, oily fume
of skunk from two rough sleepers, wind-
blown wraiths, shadows, in
a shelter on the front. Fresh print
of gull on sand. He bends above it
and sees, looking around, his own
print where he approached. Its ragged,
fluctuant track. And tries, softly
intoning, to call back a ghost.

*

Above the sound of waves, distant
rustle of scrub, faint first breeze rippling
desert steppe. Working the mind
again. Its broken door. Well-head full
of sand. Its threadbare rope that goes
clack, clack, clack. With nothing at the end
of it. Except a dusty road, white as worm-
wood under midday sun. Black shadows
on it. Chafed feet. Burnt and torn.

*

Friday night. Eviscerated black
plastic bags. Gulls scavenge
gutter and road. Pier lights
orderly, in regular sequence, wink
on a sea always changing,
always dark. Outside a corner pub
men drink and talk. Stumbling,
later, to pee in the alley behind.
They return to smoke. He glances
at them as he wanders
back to his room. Sea spray
blows into his face. Small puddles
form as he walks. Pausing only to
lift off the counter's formica top,
a cuisine not tried before,
dinner in a styrofoam box
and then to consume, its words
a pulp he spits out,
fortune's complimentary cookie.

*

Warm wind full of ghosts.
Bunch grass blowing before
a door. As white as fire
or phosphorous combustible like
the morning star. As nights draw
in travel agent windows scream:
'Depart'! Everyone packs for the sun.
And, stepping over a puddle, he can
almost smell the scent of lilac that's
to come, that will call them back
again to grill, patio, lawn. There,

punctuated by the popping of corks,
the smell of burnt flesh hovers
on warm summer nights.

When the Quinces Begin to Ripen

"The god of poetry hates those whom fortune smiles upon…
The world is a desert!"
Tu Fu

With shaking hand I lift a brush
to compose a letter to my wife. Wondering
whether it will ever reach her. Or even
if she is still alive. A sprig of dogwood
in my belt. A cherished hope.
To see her and my children again…

"Here in a half-barbarous time and country
duckweed grows thick as a man's hand.
Everywhere its deep hue deepens. Standing
at the edge of an endless waste I address
my shadow. Because there is no one else
to converse with. No calling back that wraith
whorled in the wind who haunts this margin
black with storm squall and cloud. Here
the mud stained hem's soon rinsed out.
The broken dyke restored – no crocodile found.
On roadsides the dying, for want of food,
linger. Not for us, or their kind, do the lotuses
in the imperial hot-spring gardens open
punctually each winter. As I look out across
a marsh of fragrant weeds that seems to
go on for ever, I toss a token peck of rice onto
the water in a vain attempt to appease a shadow.

Ten years now and all those years spent wandering.
A thick mist fell like smoke, they said, on
roof-tops and branches the night before
Chang'-an fell. Ominous sounds from all the wells.
Horses in the imperial stables miscarried.
The gatekeepers pawned their virtue many times
that night to a trickle of wealthy merchants.
Money flees before anyone else knows the house
is on fire. And in the inner palaces Yang Guifei
frantic for the syrup of that little god lychee
all the way from the hot south. To assuage
a halitosis compounding beauty. Who dared
place an offering of cherry, blossoming delicate
white cloud, at the ancestral shrine anymore?

A warm south wind gusts now
through the courtyard, shaking the
boughs of the quince tree, as if
it was wrestling with phantoms.
My bones ache. Damp and delirious
I turn over and over without sleeping.
All day the clinking of ice-pedlars
echoed down lane and alley: clear,
hard, cold; as if the mere sound
might allay a fever. The river thrashes
in the gorge beneath the city wall
like an animal tethered for slaughter.
Light goes and fireflies drift in and out
of the screen at the foot of the bed
as if it was a sky woven with portents.

Beneath my window a young man with one arm,
veteran of imperial adventures, pleads for alms.
In thousands of towns and villages far back from
the frontier, he tells a benefactor, nothing
grows but weeds. None are left to recruit, the old
have all flown. On the river miasmal vapours
drift. Last night, like Ming Huang, I dreamed of that
fierce eyed chaser of devils and pestilences Chung K'uei
and his dark dissolving gaze but woke, parched and wet
my forehead still burning, and lay prostrate. Must
I always wake to this: the state's derelictions and
depredations proliferate like wild grass? Outside
in the courtyard a bird sings. The quinces begin to ripen.

This fifth day of fifth moon. People wake early.
The orioles no longer call softly among the willows.
The wisteria blossoms are full. Those who can afford to
buy cakes flavoured with them. All day the poor drift through
the north gate. Cattails and catnips nailed to doors to dispel
plagues, pestilential influences. Today the God is touring
the city, in a tangled procession of images and penitents
scourging their flesh. Inspecting, in his divine excursus,
its health. As if there were an antidote to all the filth
the spirit languishes in, that might purge the source
of the distemper of this imperfect world. I hear them pass
the second sluice, and then cross the river. To
this city of dust I wonder whether they will ever return.

Perhaps there's no cure after all for what assails
us when poets, like birds in winter, flee to the
furthest corners of the earth. The gate-gods, all, are
wearied. No use plastering up their images, mere
strips of peeling yellow paper, to ward off calamity
when it has already arrived. I roll over and over.
My body fire. A dried-up inkstone in a corner,
brushes. Almost another life. Yesterday two broken
backed mules paused under my window. Their loads
a sentence to a short life. And their driver, in rags,
sullen, bare footed. There's no escaping. Greed, fear,
circumvented compassion. Part, I heard myself repeat
from the depth of delirium, of the air we breathe. Then
a bird called out. Smell of quince filled the courtyard."

Flowering Midnight
(For Mafruha)

> "She was walking like a Greek woman in Hades,
> like a Christian woman in Dante's *Inferno*, carrying
> a burden as old as History itself."
> Marguerite Yourcenar

I

Under your collar
starched by the kiss of
flatirons I could smell
a faint scent, like amaretto
or oleander. Mixed
with that of Imperial Leather.

In an arbour, *hortus voluptatis*,
under the dusty boughs
of a linden tree, reclined on
a mossed bank, I imagined
I could hear, as you described
barricades thrown up in haste
at dawn across streets,
dogs bark. "The arbour is full
of noises" you said.

Who heard the bell
that struck the hour
of that midnight feast?

Under your roving hands
fragrant with flowers
there moved, through a grey
twilight, the face of one
I was fated to meet
one drear December
on the outskirts of a city dying
of boredom and fear.

Nails driven or pulled
what was the difference
in that midnight embrace
where solace was not
offered or asked for
and the heart wore
a tattered leaf shadow
a young girl's dress.

In the tedium
of unheated boudoirs
at midnight, cold
and disconsolate,
I counted the hours
waiting for you to arrive,
that sour spittle on your lip
a grape, your leg heavy
as a clod over mine.
A childhood of unassuaged
imaginings wrapped round
your little finger.

In darkness, I began
to suspect, only
did you truly open. Corolla
of empty slogan, cliché, catechism,
lullaby. A closed book:
to the inamorata in the ruined
garden, her vagabond
ghost sucking the dark
bitter pith of its fruit.
In a library of clear water,
a fountain, I saw your
inconsolable expression, heard
you mourning amidst the
apocrypha of each new dawn.

You came, slowly,
to resemble a blind man
stumbling amid ruins
of a past you did not understand.
As if you had dreamed it.
As if the pain of not being
there, in that *locus periucundus*, could
be quenched by tormenting another.
You expected me to dance
amid scattered spolia
to the faded choreography
of an illusion and to sing
to you like a fountain.
A dark ditch, rather,
to irrigate festering roses.

Days spent years later, after you
left on another fundraising and tour,
at the creek head. In a cloud
of mosquitoes, looking at water. Lights
flickered on and off at the shoreline. Then
stayed off: prison and army barracks
exhausting the grid with demands.
Night mingled the cry of victim
and sound of nightingale-thrush.
Over jagged inlet, wetland they floated.
Pain of convulsed limbs, torso
strapped down, merged with acme of
avian ardour. Some listened, offended
disturbed. Most did not.

You were midnight, I realised.
All along. In so many guises, places
and times. In seas of suffocating steerage
and oblivion. In plantations
of immense cruelty. Disavowed.
Your spoor, always changing
always the same. Towards the end
whenever you spoke in that high
pained voice you had perfected over
the years, of pique, irritable
opprobrium, I would hear the rattle
in drawing rooms of glass cabinets
opening. Full of antiques. Smell the stale
pomade of antimacassars eternally
whitening. You were like, I thought,

the old organ grinder on the corner
grinding out, year after year, the same
sad tune. Always, it seemed, at dusk.
On his threadbare clothes, as I passed,
I would smell the same sickly sweet
odour of roses that had never opened.

In a dusk of wood pigeons
and dust caked bowls of silent
fountains of an indebted estate,
on a bed of leaves beneath a tree
full of rotting oranges, they
(gardener and helpmate from
whom the rumour, soon scotched,
entered neighbouring towns)
had come upon you.
In flagrante delicto.
Thrusting, beneath the stained
tearings of a young girl's
dress, and groaning.
Your 'right': to demand
from an indigent's sirings
the youngest and earliest fruit
to spoil, in lui of confiscation
of all he possessed. For which
no doubt later you would return:
your kind never getting enough.

II

Bright spurge and amaryllis.
A fragrant surrogate, an *arbor
Paradisi*, runs through all our days.
And like love, an old love, is, O
an old sore. Worked up,
under the collar, into
a poisonous malaise, it spreads.
Whored to prosperity, a bankrupt
pastoral: to the dictatorship of the rich.

III

I remembered days when he'd come back
smelling like a bunch of sweet grass:
dust of road, culm, attached
to him. Hand sweat tasting of
leather. Oil and unguent could erase
palm scars scored by reins. Redress
ravages of wind, sun. Too deep, though,
for them to erase, that shadow
midnight drew through my life. And draws
through the life of each of us and which,
like fallen angels, we can neither flee nor
acknowledge. Too deep for them, too,
to erase, that sound of dogs
tearing flesh in the scented arbour.
Delivered to them each day
until they'd developed a taste for it.
Staked out for them. Still remonstrating:
while musicians played and ladies

under parasols, sipping cool
cordials, chattered and applauded.

He was my *daemon meridianus*
coming to lie with me,
"spell-stopp'd",
under the linden tree
in the cool breeze
bearing the scent of flowers
and incense. A dark breath-
ed censer dispensing endearments
into my heart. Bondage. Not bower.

And he was my north
ima praecipitari
turned into my south.
Wherever I turned to look
midnight masqueraded as dawn.
My true alignment became north.
So much so that night
deepened and whitened about me
removing 'impurities', 'stains'. All
opposites dissolved. A winnowing
of voices. Only his,
white cantor, dark tongue,
could be heard.

Under his collar,
halter, greasy white noose,
I inserted, at last, thumbs
and fingers and pulled. Tight. Till
those words liberté, égalité, fraternité,
sepulchres for bleeding ghosts,
choked in his throat. Saying:
"Broken philosophe, apothecary
no poultice, no potion, no salve
for the wound? Try this
garrot slowly turned, by one
of those with two legs
your kind first herded, penned."

From Tide Washed Salterns

"So sweet a smell … as if we had bene
in the midst of some delicate garden."

Arthur Barlowe *The Roanoke Voyages 1584–1590*

On salt eaten quays
beside dark copses of alders
in the midday heat of a false
summer, who will deliver them
from their transgressions
their restless stratagems and
narrow tyrannies: latter day heroes
mouthing cruel platitudes of their
congeners. From the submerged
chapel at the shoreline, from
the miry track from the ferry
leading northward, pilgrims
with their pyxides of holy water,
loud-talking, they went
seeking the ideal city
"lusting for it like pigs" to far
off isles, dispensing terror,
signing their names
in the black smoke of ruins,
not looking back – to tide washed, wild
flower salterns littered with
cracked brine pans where barges
were hovelled wharfwards, to
angled bastions of old Dutch
embankments where first Spring
droughts baked the creeks' ditch
hollows and driftways

iron hard, to quiet deliberations
by which they were found wanting.

When they returned they moved
amongst us as if nothing had happened
out of the ordinary course of events
displaying mementoes of far places
brass fingerbowls, flagons, ceremonial
scabbards, buffed and buffed
until they glowed in dark sculleries,
on staircases. Who, now, will
redeem them: from their violent
intolerance and ways? From
salt fretted wastes they troop still
down the centuries. Like ghosts
returning to roost they enter
our streets and houses,
propounding old platitudes
refurbished but the same.
In the smoking ruins
of a dream endlessly intoning
them, old men with a hard
intemperate gaze, they wait.
Sea asters droop now
beside derelict quays
at the creek heads
in the first Spring droughts.
Out of the cracked earth
an exhausted incubus rises.

The Carved Serpent

"Oh flowering futility of the world …"
Tasos Leivaditis *The Scent of the Night*

    Snow falls. Moment
    by moment. Carpeting
    the black thorn porch
    of a church, serpent coiled
    but repulsed, and a higgledy
    piggledy main street
    working its way up from
    the marsh. A dark music
    fills the air. In a ploughed
    field a battered cuirass
    buried for centuries
    begins to emerge. A bird sings
    in the alder trees beside
    the road. Nightlong it sings.

    You lie awake.
    Listening for the sound
    of a thaw. Roads
    impassable. Wind. History
    is a dark field ploughed
    again and again,
    harvest we cannot atone
    for. Ghost acreages
    tilled by invisible hands.
    And this snow, falling
    and falling.

    In a dream you stumble
    through deep drifts.

From farmstead
to ruined farmstead.
A broken compass
in your hand. *In how many
guises do you appear
before us, make yourself
known to us?* All the embankments
eroded. The churchyard
a bare mound. No footprint
but the wind's. And
the chimeras, *We were
slothful and
inattentive ... Who, now,
should we accuse if
not ourseleves?*, are
gathering again in the
black thorn porch.
In an alder tree
beside the road
a bird is singing.

Night

"I have come to lead you to the other shore;
into eternal darkness, into fire and into ice."

Dante *Inferno*: [III: 86-87]

Faint mist over the salt marsh.
Broken-up horizon. Jib and boom.
Wharves given over to trinkets.
Roadways full of those
with an entranced gaze
heading off into the future.
At frostbitten terminals
and quays they breathe, in a city
in whose overgrown parks and weed-
locked sidings the homeless
each night lay their heads,
a twilight of contaminated moments

Like light, disinterring at end
of day each rufous tint
entombed in sandstone wall,
night collects you. Fragment
upon uneasy fragment. Collects
what can't be counted or
observed beyond the act of counting
and collating. What is forged
in a moment of surrender, after
the moment has extinguished itself.

Evening. Warm with a wind
of tar and oil off
the river. In a ruined garden
under willow and aspen
afloat on the debris of all
lived moments, fireflies rise
and fall, ignite and die
in the scented dusk
beneath the trees. You stand,
for a while, watching
the slow interstitial ebb
and flow of their light.
Moment by moment. Adrift
on the current of fire that
moves through everything. That
everything moves toward
in a moment of surrender.

Forsaken, primordial moment.
No returning to where the path
was lost on an afternoon you have
forgotten. Overcast and shrouded
in drizzle. Caught between two states
comprehending, fully, neither.

*On the cold stones of an ambrosial
coast, having sacrificed nothing
and given up everything,
they place their feet. Over the salt marsh,
burying that "old mongrel world"
of latchgate and driftway
that pre-technoparadiso,
the snow lies deep. Lights
on quay and terminal,
through thickly falling flakes,
flash. On. Off. On. Off. Like
fireflies under blossoming trees.*

At the time before mind
asserted itself over the tumult
of all successive moments:
weaving a pattern, keeping
it alive in that continuous
thread of overlapping instants
parting, re-joining. Knitting
them up. When sitting alone at
the window. When scent of phlox
from the garden entered the room.
When you neither heard what
was said, nor appeared to listen
your mind alert only to that
unrecovered moment into which
history had not inserted itself.

*On the unkempt corner of a street, time of edicts
and false proclamations, the future breaks
against them: in sabotaged out-of-work towns
of blackened brickwork. In small stores boarded up,
bankrupted lives. The bookshops all gone.
Word-hoard held in a cloud. No longer burned
but, like memory, deleted. As they stand there,
"material for an inhuman experiment", snow falls
again on everything. The frozen kerbside.
Yesterday. Tomorrow. Great blank, the coldest
and whitest of all incunabulas, descending
on time's fevered formations, insignia. And no port any
longer for them to turn to, outrunning the storm.*

And the pattern, that
an instant shatters and
repairs, becomes an end
in itself. And the path,
on an afternoon you have
forgotten, can't be restored.
Imposed upon each
living moment, woven in
the flesh: a pattern. Settling
on inlet and embankment
in a twilight of mist and rain.
Until you, conjured from
the debris of all lived
moments, cannot tell where
it and you begin, end.

Nostos

Always it is the same. History
is a handful of tired pieties, predilections:
animosities of attachment of grasper
and grasped. Affirming a transitory
and tenuous existence, the plenitude
of a present which cannot last. And
its last moment is also its first
in an infinite series of moments renewed.

The diffused aromas of a lost
summer hover around a faded grey
gatepost in a field. Discarded
fragments of a life surrendered.
One to come: beyond this moment,
hesitant, but sure. One, the spider
spinning in the wainscot a new
death and a beginning for us, we are
reluctant, mired in the immense nostalgia
for all lost moments, to forgo.

***

"In my hours of gloom ... what is left for me but to seek out the true, lost face of music somewhere off in the forest ... among the birds."

Olivier Messiaen

[From Preface to score of *Quartet for the End of Time* composed and first performed in Stalag 8-A, 1941]

***

Acknowledgements

To the editors of the following magazines and reviews in the Philippines, Hong Kong, Canada, USA, Austria and UK in which these poems, and in some cases earlier versions of them, first appeared: *Antigonish Review; Fire; High Chair; Imprint; Iron; Longhouse; Ninth Decade; O.Ars; Oasis; Other Poetry; Palantir; Paper Air; Poetry Salzburg Review; Prism International; Shearsman; Sulfur; Tamarisk; Tenth Decade; The Philippine Graphic; The Journal; Tremblestone; Waves; West Coast Review; Wheatear.*

My thanks to Leung Lo Yu whose help with the translations from Chinese was indispensable.

~

Also my thanks to David Wevill whose expressed and keen appreciation of many of these poems galvanized me into collecting them. And to Tony Frazer for his enduring support of my work.

Poems in this volume appeared, sometimes in different form, in the following publications: *The Kneeling Room* (Blue Guitar Books, Plymouth, 1981), *The Ash Circle* (Shearsman Books, Plymouth, 1986; revised edition: Alms House Press, New York, 1989), *Heard Lanes* (Alms House Press, New York, 1989), *Dried Flowers* (Alms House Press, New York, 1990), *Swamp Fever* (Willamette River Books, Troutdale, OR, 1991), *The Stillness of Gardens* (Willamette River Books, Troutdale, OR, 1994), *Black Confetti* (University of the Philippines Press, Diliman, 1999), *Three Poems* (Oasis Books, London, 2002), *Belonging* (Shearsman Books, Exeter, 2009), *Interlocutors of Paradise* (Skylight Press, Cheltenham, 2012), *Obsequy for Lost Things* (Shearsman Books, Bristol, 2014), *Ice Stylus* (Shearsman Books, Bristol, 2017), *In the Empire of Chimeras* (Shearsman Books, Bristol, 2018), *A Country Without Names* (Shearsman Books, Bristol, 2022).

Notes

THE STILLNESS OF GARDENS

Page 128. David Jones in *The Anathémata* refers to the Chase in Corringham: "The discovery of skulls and other bones of oxen under St. Paul's in 1316 assisted a traditional belief that the site had once been sacred to Diana. On the feast of the commemoration of St. Paul, June 30th, the dean and chapter zoomorphically vested and crowned with roses, received a buck from the deer-park of Curingham [sic] in Essex."

BLACK CONFETTI

Page 169. Returning to Manila in Linda Panlilio's private jet in 1995 from the national writers' workshop in Baguio with the Filipino novelist N.V.M. Gonzalez. Before this Gonzalez had spent many years living and teaching at universities in the USA prior to returning for good to the Philippines.

UNSUBDUED SINGING TRILOGY

In the original texts of all three books (*Interlocutors of Paradise / Obsequy for Lost Things / Ice Stylus*) which comprise this trilogy, each section (titled, numbered or asterisked) appeared on a separate page.

The *English* Boat

Title

Andrew Marvell, *Bermudas*.

Farewell to the Shade

Title. William Cowper, *The Poplar-Field*.

Kaah-Kaah-Kaah

Line 7. Oliver Cromwell.

Line 7-9. Edmund Spenser, *A View of the State of Ireland*.
Line 9. *Res nullius* – Roman law by which all unoccupied or under utilized lands remained common property of mankind. Primary argument used in planting Munster and Ards. Iterated in John Locke's *The Second Treatise of Civil Government*.
Line 10. Richard Hadsor, *Discourse on the Irish State*.
Line 11-12. Edmund Spenser, *op.cit*.
Line 12. Sir William Herbert *Croftus Sive de Hibernia Liber*.

To Get the Pearl and Gold

Title. Michael Drayton, *To the Virginia Voyage*.
Line 2. Arthur Barlowe, *The Roanoke Voyages 1584–1590. Documents to Illustrate the English Voyages to North America Under the Patent Granted to Walter Ralegh in 1584*.
Line 7. Michael Drayton, *op.cit*.
Line 8-9. Arthur Barlowe, *op.cit*.
Line 13-14. Prince Henry eldest son of James 1st (Referring to Sir Walter Ralegh).
Line 19. Edmund Spenser, *Colin Clout*. (Referring to Elizabeth 1st and to Ralegh's poem [*The Ocean to*] *Scinthia* addressed to the Queen, but never circulated).
Line 21. Joseph Conrad, *Heart of Darkness*.

Out in the Open

Line 17-19. Board of Agriculture Report quoted by Christopher Hill in *Reformation to Industrial Revolution*.

A Place Insufficiently Imagined

Line 2-3. Edward Terry, as quoted in Samuel Purchas '*Hakluytus Postumus or Purchas His Pilgrimes*'.
Line 9. Attributed to Warren Hastings. "Seven entire battalions were added to our military establishment to enforce the collections … [that]carried terror and ruin through the country": Robert Orme, official historiographer of the East India Company. Orme resigned in protest in 1762.
Line 11-13. Christopher Hill, *Reformation to Industrial Revolution*.
Line 14-15. Nicholas Dirks, *The Scandal of Empire*.

Customs / Duties

Line 8-9. Chinese Government Proclamation (1810).
Line 11. Lord Palmerston: referring to Hong Kong.
Line 12-14. Commissioner Lin Zexu; *letter (1839) to Queen Victoria.*
Line 14-15. Tu Fu, *Autumn Meditation.*

Diomedea Exulans

Line 8. Herman Melville, *Moby-Dick.*

Home

Line 7-8. S.T. Coleridge, *Rime of the Ancient Mariner*

City of Flowering Almonds

Page 230. Joseph Conrad, *Heart of Darkness.*
    Bernardino de Sahagún, *The Florentine Codex.*
Page 231. Sir Walter Ralegh, *As you came from the holy land.*
Page 232. Joachim Gaunse: prominent Jewish Czech mining engineer and metallurgist recruited by Sir Walter Ralegh for his Virginia expedition.
Page 232. Edward Gibbon, *The History of the Decline and Fall of the Roman Empire.*
Page 233. From exercises found at Nippur (circa 1,800 BCE) used in the learning of Sumerian.
Ezra Pound, *Hugh Selwyn Mauberley.*
Page 233. Sir John Tyrell, *Ancient Wills* (Essex Archaeological Society Transactions).
Page 234. Cole Porter, *Blue Moon.*
Page 234. Christopher Columbus, *Journal* (3rd voyage).
Page 234. Sir Walter Ralegh, *The Discovery of Guiana 1595.*
Arthur Barlowe, *The Roanoke Voyages 1584–1590. Documents to Illustrate the English Voyages to North America Under the Patent Granted to Walter Ralegh in 1594.*

Ethnological Curiosities

Page 236. J.S. Mill, *On Liberty* (paraphrasing Jeremy Bentham).
Page 239. Rabindranath Tagore, *The Modern Age.*

Between the River and the Sea

Page 243. King James 1st of England. *Royal Patent* of the Virginia Company.
Page 244. *Periplus Maris Erythraei.*
Page 245. Joseph Banks, *Correspondence.*
Page 246. A.R. Wallace, *The Origin of Human Races.*

The Bee Wood

Page 247. **medhu.* Proto-Indo-European for 'honey'; also 'mead'. *melitos.* Greek for 'honey'.
Page 247. **bha-l-tos.* Proto-Indo-European for 'shining white'. Later in Lithuanian *baltas* and Latvian *balts* > people living in the white snow lands.
From the *Epic of Gilgamesh*: "I entered the house of dust and I saw the kings of the earth, their crowns put away for ever".
Page 248 *sal* > Sanskrit for 'to move about' from Proto-Indo-European *sel* in **selyenes,* a dancing, tripping, marching people > appearing later in Greek as *Hellenes,* a people who entered the area of Greece around second millennium BCE.
"1786" > date of William Jones' announcement to the Royal Asiatick Society of his discovery, *pace* Sanskrit, of the Indo European language pool; suggesting a source, other than Hebrew, for the 'original' Adamic language which predated the pluralism of Babel.
Page 249. "Inessential houses". From *The Great Gatsby*, Scott Fitzgerald.
Page 249. From Linnaeus's taxonomy of races in his *Systema Naturae* (1753).
Page 250. "Refugees from dust". From *The Grapes of Wrath,* John Steinbeck.
Page 250. "The same monsters, the same longings" pursued by "men of inconstancy, of wanderings and of wars" such as Odysseus. From George Seferis's 'A Letter on 'Thrush'.

The Lower Reaches

One

I: "We'll bomb ..", Pakistan's President Musharraf, BBC television interview, 2006. Threat made to him by US official. [First used by American General Curtis LeMay in 1968 in relation to N. Vietnam.]

IV: "Die ..", from target photographs of Thameshaven oil refineries issued to Luftwaffe aircrews during WWII.
"Zu den ..", Edmund Husserl, *Logische Untersuchungen*, 1900/01. [We

must turn to the things themselves! – Rather than, as in Kant, the mystical thing-in-itself.]

V: "Outside the window ..", following the Great North Sea Flood of 1953, in which many people drowned, Fobbing's navigable tideway was, in the interests of safety, dammed off and its creek eventually dried out.
"leakinge, unwholesome ..", John Smith, *The Generall History of Virginia, New England, and the Summer Isles*, 1624: Smith's description is of the *Mayflower*.
"Sea-mark", Randal Bingley, *Fobbing: Essays on an Essex Parish*.

VI: Togodumnus: a king of the Catuvellauni in southern England who, in a battle described as one of the most important in English history and which might have taken place between present day East Tilbury and Stanford-le-Hope, resisted the Roman invasion / occupation (CE43) and who was 'lost' "retreating into trackless wastes" of the Essex marshes and became, Hind claims, a client king.

VII: "a perpetuall ..", Virginia Company *Records* vol.1, 1622. [By 1685 the Powhatans of the Chesapeake tidelands were reportedly 'extinct']. "(save upward ..", William Bradford first Governor of Plymouth, New England, 1620, *Of Plymouth Plantation*.

Two

I: "Hole Haven ..", inlet on the Thames estuary 'traditionally serving as a minor harbour for sea-going vessels' (Bingley). A place much visited, especially its *Lobster Smack Inn*, by the novelist Joseph Conrad's lifelong friend G.W.F. Hope, who along with Conrad lived at one time in Stanford-le-Hope, an Essex village on the banks of the Thames a couple of miles from Hole Haven. Hope, in his *Friend of Conrad* (1926), describes it: "The next day we went aboard the *Nellie*, taking with us a cold leg of lamb ... we got down to the Lower Hope reach. We passed several sailing ships and steamers as we made our way down to Hole Haven. When we got near the Haven I told Conrad I would take the foresail in and to keep her well down to the sea wall so as not to run any risk of touching the spit as we approached the creek. We had a fair wind in, so I lowered the main sail and took in the mizzen. We then ran up above the jetty, and let go the anchor just inside the eel schoots. We then stowed the sails and brought forth the lamb". In

Hope's manuscript he identifies himself as the 'Director' in Conrad's *Heart of Darkness*, an extract from which precedes this description.

II: *Der Angriff*, newspaper published by Joseph Goebbels.
Robert Conway, main protagonist in the Frank Capra film *Lost Horizon* 1937.
"that nobly ..", Charles White, *An Account of the Regular Graduations in Man*,1799 [White in his account was referring to Europeans].

V: "For a ..", Eric J. Dolin, *Fur, Fortune and Empire*.
"beaver fields ..", *Jesuits Relations*, 1635 [from an estimated population of 60+ million beavers].

VI: This entire section indebted to J.F. Hind's *A Plautius' Campaign in Britain. An Alternative Reading of the Narrative in Cassius Dio (60.19.5-21.2)*
"in avia ..", retreating into trackless wastes, *op.cit.*
"REG MAG ..", Great King in Britain, *op.cit.*
"reges et ..", compliant, friendly kings, *op.cit.*

VII: "aguish miasma", William Gibbens, *The Essex Review*, 1902.

VIII: 'Big swinging ..', term denoting a City of London floor trader.
"A culture ..", Adair Turner, Financial Services Authority, London, June 2012.

IX: "cultivated ..", Eduardo Galeano, *Open Veins of Latin America*. ["The powerful who legitimate their privileges by heredity cultivate nostalgia."]
"swear all ..", Roland Huntford, *Shackleton*. [Referring to Robert Falcon Scott].

X: "From le ..", circa 1263, Randal Bingley, *op.cit.* [Hole Haven was also known as Holy Haven.]
"in very ..", *National Archives*, Kew, United Kingdom. [Relating to "purged" Kenya files. Those involved in such purging were required to be "a British subject of *European descent*."] Italics mine.
"perambulation", Randal Bingley, *op.cit.*
"by the ..", an unnamed settler of the *Kenyan Police Reserve* who participated in a Special Branch interrogation: "Stayed for a few hours to help the boys out, softening him up ...". Interviewed and

cited by C. Elkins, *Britain's Gulag: the Brutal End of Empire in Kenya*.
"Bounds of ..", Randal Bingley, *op.cit.*
"might embarrass ..", Ian MacLeod, UK Secretary of State for the Colonies, 1961.
"he died ..", C. Elkins, *op.cit.*

Ice Stylus

In physics the zone of middle dimensions, according to physicist Fritjof Capra, is where the mechanistic view of classical physics – that of empty space and of solid material bodies moving through it – continues to be of use and is deeply ingrained in our thought. Just as this view is not the view of sub-atomic physicists, so the conventional view of perception – that of space filled with material bodies which exist independently of us – is not the view of Mahayana Buddhists. Even though Mahayana thinkers would admit the utility of such a deeply ingrained view, samvrti-satya, they would not endorse its veracity.

Unsubdued Singing

Terms for toponomy and hydronomy are the most durable designations within landscape and form the most stable substratum of linguistic evidence for the identity of human habitation. Numerous indigenous river names in North America, however, were sacrificed to that of the River Thames (page 236) in England. In England its name, significantly, survived the depredations of Roman, Saxon, Dane, Norman and probably (since we know the cognate for it in Sanskrit) Celt.

A COUNTRY WITHOUT NAMES

The cover image for the original book was a Luftwaffe photograph of the September 1940 bombing of Thameshaven oil refineries. The inlet of Hole Haven (bottom left of the photograph) on Fobbing Marsh in the Lower Hope region of the Thames, where the *Nellie* in Joseph Conrad's *Heart of Darkness* was moored close to the Chapman lighthouse, is obscured by thick smoke; but not the rest of the creek meandering, in a north north easterly direction, towards the foot of Fobbing village.

The title page image is of a bird emitting sounds depicted as glyphs and carved speech scrolls forming logographs. It is from the rollout drawing of the excised design of an Olmec stamp from San Andrés, Tabasco, Mexico.

Epigraph

Nightingales: as of 2018 their numbers had diminished in the UK, along with numerous other bird species, by over 90%.

Dedication

An English Master who in the words of Horace *"carminis nomenque dedit poetae"*: you have conferred on me the name of poet. His friend, the poet Martin Bell, penned for him this memorable quatrain:

Prospect 1939 *(For Campbell Matthews)*

'Life is a journey' said our education.
And so we packed, although we found it slow.
At twenty one, left stranded at the station,
We've heaps of luggage and nowhere to go.

Rock Star Celebrates Birthday at Exclusive Country House Retreat

Quotation in the text: Ben Jonson *To Penshurst*

Road to the North

FIRE: acronym for the Finance, Insurance and Real Estate sector which accounts for most increases in wealth in modern western capitalism.
House of Finance: the Mithraic remains are preserved in London in the basement of the headquarters of the American financial-data giant Bloomberg.
Turnpikes: Henry VII's 1489 act 'Agaynst the Pulling Doun of Touns'.

Quotations in the text in order:
UK National Archives (re: Kenya) Kew; Sir Charles Noble Arden-Clarke (Gold Coast); Epic of Gilgamesh; Isaac Walton.

Alder

In Lapp the word 'lei'be' denoting the alder tree also denotes menstrual blood and bear's blood, constituting an etymological site where pre-Neolithic, and early Neolithic, beliefs are preserved.

Where No Snow Falls

Quotation in the text: from the Greek epic *Odyssey*... According to classicist Rhys Carpenter, Salmoxis, a Thracian god of immortality and said to have worn a bear skin, provided the thematic material, of prolonged disappearance and sudden reappearance, for the poem composed during a period of early Greek mercantilist expansion in the Mediterranean. The kind of immortality which Salmoxis represented, however, was not the "deathless immortality" of the Olympians (or lesser state of rejuvenescence which Athena bestows upon that returned and ageing Hero who the poet George Seferis characterised as a man "of inconstancy, of wanderings and of wars") but the older palingenesis of life, death and new life which the disappearing and reappearing bear, as master of renewal and the wheel of seasons, emerging just ahead of the snow melt with her young, appeared to embody. Telemachus, son of Odysseus, refers to his grandfather as Arkeisius, "bear son", the result of Cephalus mating with a she-bear, confirming the ancient matrilineal and Pre-Indo European myth of a line founded by bear-human marriage.

Reliquary

Quotation in the text: the Buddhist logician Nagarjuna.

Road of Dust

The road of the title refers to that leading to Kaifeng where Li Yu, poet, musician, painter, devout Buddhist and last emperor of the Southern Tang Dynasty, was transported after Taizu's army's protracted investiture of his capital city Nanjing (Jinling) which, in the winter of 976 CE, finally fell. For years Taizu, emperor of the subsequent Sung Dynasty, had conducted an aggressive military policy of intimidation, destabilisation and invasion of independent minded states in an attempt to bring all of them and their resources under his control. The Southern Tang state was the last to succumb.

In Chinese Buddhism dust refers to the realms of the six sense faculties, consciousness regarded as one of them. Hence 'dust-consciousness'. Such consciousness, likened to the bustle and sensory allure of a marketplace, is seen to obscure the underlying nature of perception.

Quotation in the text: the Buddhist logician Nagarjuna.

Under Jiu-yi Shan

Regarded as the 'father' of Chinese poetry and whose foundational poem *Li Sao* struck a clear political note of dissent: "Let us be clear: it is hopeless! The state has no statesman." Ch'u Yuan was a leading minister in the State of Chu (the same state in which during the Warring States period Lao Tzu author of the *Tao Teh Ching* was born) during the fourth and third century BCE; a time, like today, of remorseless wars. Because of court rivalries, "Day and night they curse and vilify me", and of his hostility to the growing power of the State of Chin, a Legalist highly centralised and authoritarian state (similar to, in the West, Justinian's Christian state) which would give its name to the region we now identify as China, he was exiled south to a non-Sinitic culture and region, present day Hunan, where he traversed ceaselessly the vast undrained swamps and wetlands around the Dongting lakes: "I weep for sweet herbs among foul weeds ... With trembling heart I wander the marshlands." His famous long poem *Li Sao* (Encountering Sorrow) was profoundly influenced by the shamanistic songs and lore of the region. His death by his own hand in the Miluo River is commemorated, each fifth day of the fifth month of the traditional lunisolar calendar, by the dragon boat festival. The dragon on the boat prow is a motif which derives from the crocodile. *Under Jiu-yi Shan* (Nine Doubt Mountain, a site in southern Hunan sacred as the burial place of Shun one of the most revered rulers of antiquity noted for his moral stature) embeds various lines from *Li Sao* and observations on Ch'u Yuan by Su-ma Ch'ien the Great Recorder of the first century BCE.

A Country Without Names

Quotations in the text in order: Thomas Jefferson, Edward Gibbon, George Seferis.

When the Quinces Begin to Ripen

Tu Fu was a very minor official in the Chinese capital Chang'-an in the northern part of the country. A rebellion by An Lu-shan in 755 captured the capital and very nearly ended the Tang dynasty. Tu Fu, who was not there at the time, was taken prisoner by the rebels and taken to Chang'-an. He eventually escaped and joined the imperial court and was rewarded with a higher position on its return to Chang'-an. But he was far too outspoken, especially on issues of social justice, for his own good and was, fortunately, only demoted. He was posted to a minor position in an out of the way location. It was perhaps during this time, or sometime later, he contracted malaria. Eventually, after many enforced wanderings over what had become an unstable country where the rebellion spawned many other rebellions for many years, he retired and in 766 arrived and lived the last years of his life in K'uei-chou in the far southern region of Hunan where the poet Ch'u Yuan ("that wraith") had, many centuries before, been exiled. He stayed there for two years, bitterly lamenting his "failure in a ruined Empire". Attempting to set off north again for his birthplace with, finally, his family, perhaps in response to another rebellion brewing nearby, he died whilst still in Hunan.

Emperor Ming-huang (712–756) suffering from a fever went to sleep and in a dream was tormented by a demon. Suddenly the imposing figure of Chung K'uei appeared in his dream and killed the demon. On waking the emperor's fever had gone and he subsequently canonised Chung K'uei as: "Great Spiritual Chaser of Demons for the Whole Empire".

Yang Guifei was the young wife of the Emperor Ming-huang.

[Some degree of sentiment regarding use of Chinese names employing the Wade-Giles system of Romanisation has led, in the 'Chinese' poems and the Notes, to inconsistencies. Having for almost half a century lived with, for instance, Tu Fu as phonologically just that I have not wished to jettison it for the now more generally used *Du Fu*. Other names, using the official Pin-yin system, having come upon them only relatively recently, I have had no such qualms about. The original Wade-Giles forms, however, in which some names first presented themselves to me all those years ago, have been retained.]

From Tide Washed Salterns

Quotation in the text: Bernardino de Sahagún *The Florentine Codex*.

Night

Quotations in the text in order: Alexander Blok *The Twelve*; Maxim Gorky *The New Life*.

www.ingramcontent.com/pod-product-compliance
Lightning Source LLC
Chambersburg PA
CBHW021758220426
43662CB00006B/109